Django 5 Cookbook

Over 70+ problem solving techniques, sample programs, and troubleshoots across python programs and web apps

Clara Stein

Published by: GitforGits

Publisher: Sonal Dhandre

www.gitforgits.com

support@gitforgits.com

Printed in India

First Printing: March 2024

ISBN: 9788119177677

Cover Design by: Kitten Publishing

Prologue

In the bustling world of technology, where the landscape of web development evolves at an astonishing pace, I found myself at the crossroads of innovation and tradition. Having spent a considerable amount of time learning Python and Django, I can attest to the fact that these languages are truly remarkable for the way they can give life to ideas. I set out on this technical problem solving project with the intention of producing more than simply a learning book. With its focus on real-world recipes, this book captures the essence of Django, covering everything from the basics of setting up a working environment to the architectural marvels of constructing scalable web applications. Each chapter demonstrates Django's power and versatility through an underlying story that connects the basic ideas and advanced features.

An imaginary web app called GitforGits is the backbone of this book and the medium through which we investigate it. As it progresses, readers will face situations and obstacles that are similar to those in real-world projects, providing a realistic view of how to use Django's capabilities. This practical approach guarantees that the information shared, can be instantly put into practice, enabling readers to utilize Django's potential in their own projects.

The book is filled with Django's guiding principles, which promote quick development and practical, clean design. By highlighting the importance of security best practices, performance optimization, and the DRY principle, I am trying to cultivate a mindset that prioritizes efficiency, maintainability, and robustness. As an example of how Django fits nicely with the modern development ecosystem, consider its interaction with front-end technologies like React.js and Vue.js, containerization with Docker, orchestration with Kubernetes, and the installation of CI/CD pipelines.

When development is rushed, security, which is an essential component that is frequently neglected, is given the attention it deserves. To help readers protect their applications from the many online dangers, this book includes recipes on how to secure Django APIs, how to implement token authentication, and how to use Django's natural security capabilities. To further strengthen this security posture, Prometheus monitoring and logging can be used to gain insights into the activity and health of applications.

The strength of open-source software and the community that supports it is demonstrated in this book, which is more than simply a collection of recipes. Whether you're an experienced developer seeking to improve your expertise or a complete beginner ready to dive headfirst into the exciting world of web development, this book will serve as a guiding light, providing insights, inspiration, and practical advice without being a long and heavily filled book.

My goal in writing this book was to make web development easier to understand and use, and to introduce Django to anyone interested in its capabilities. I am very delighted to have you along for this thrilling adventure of exploration, education, and creativity. Let's explore Django together, creating not only apps but a future where technology may have a constructive impact.

Prologue

Content

Preface

For Python programmers, backend developers, and web developers looking to become experts in the Django framework and improve their problem-solving skills, "Django 5 Cookbook" is the simplest and easiest pocket solution book. This book presents a variety of recipes and solutions to the complex problems of developing web applications in a clear and concise manner. Presented in a logical progression from basic ideas to more complex implementations, this book covers every angle when it comes to Django.

The first step in building powerful web apps is learning how to set up Django in a virtual environment. Models, databases, user interfaces, and authentication are all thoroughly covered as the script goes along, providing a strong groundwork for creating fast and secure applications. Django REST Framework integration with popular front-end frameworks like React.js and Vue.js, as well as the development of flexible APIs, are all covered in detail with sample programs.

Chapters on CI/CD, logging with Prometheus, and safeguarding Django APIs highlight the significance of best practices in software development, while containerization with Docker and orchestration with Kubernetes simplify the deployment of scalable applications.

"Django 5 Cookbook" is more than just a collection of solutions; it's a guide for those who want to become skilled Django developers and problem solvers. Not only will readers have a firm grasp of Django by the book's conclusion, but they will also have internalized the mindset necessary to build web applications that are secure, easy to maintain, and of high quality, enabling them to confidently face the challenges of their daily jobs.

In this book you will learn:

- Learn Django setup and settings for cross-environment development.
- Master Django's ORM to efficiently manage database operations.
- Use forms and authentication to create engaging user interfaces.
- Use Django REST Framework to create flexible, scalable APIs.
- Build dynamic web apps with integrating Django to React.js or Vue.js.
- Use Docker and Kubernetes to standardize development and production.
- Build faster with CI/CD's automated testing and deployment.
- Implement strong Prometheus logging strategies for real-time application monitoring and troubleshooting.
- Optimize Django performance by scaling easily with distributed systems.
- Enhance Django API security to avoid vulnerabilities and threats.

GitforGits

Prerequisites

Web developers, backend engineers, and Python programmers who want to learn the ins and outs of the Django framework and become better problem solvers will love this book. It is ideal if you know the basics of working with Django and Python scripting.

Codes Usage

Are you in need of some helpful code examples to assist you in your programming and documentation? Look no further! Our book offers a wealth of supplemental material, including code examples and exercises.

Not only is this book here to aid you in getting your job done, but you have our permission to use the example code in your programs and documentation. However, please note that if you are reproducing a significant portion of the code, we do require you to contact us for permission.

But don't worry, using several chunks of code from this book in your program or answering a question by citing our book and quoting example code does not require permission. But if you do choose to give credit, an attribution typically includes the title, author, publisher, and ISBN. For example, "Django 5 Cookbook by Clara Stein".

If you are unsure whether your intended use of the code examples falls under fair use or the permissions outlined above, please do not hesitate to reach out to us at support@gitforgits.com.

We are happy to assist and clarify any concerns.

Acknowledgement

I owe a tremendous debt of gratitude to GitforGits, for their unflagging enthusiasm and wise counsel throughout the entire process of writing this book. Their knowledge and careful editing helped make sure the piece was useful for people of all reading levels and comprehension skills. In addition, I'd like to thank everyone involved in the publishing process for their efforts in making this book a reality. Their efforts, from copyediting to advertising, made the project what it is today.

Finally, I'd like to express my gratitude to everyone who has shown me unconditional love and encouragement throughout my life. Their support was crucial to the completion of this book. I appreciate your help with this endeavour and your continued interest in my career.

Acknowledgements

[illegible]

[illegible]

Chapter 1: Up and Running With Django

Introduction

Starting with this chapter will help you get started with Django by giving you the tools and information you need to start making web apps. In this chapter, we will take a look at the basics of installing and configuring Django in a way that promotes best practices and a stable development environment.

The significance of isolated environments for Python projects will be highlighted when we begin with Installing Django in a Virtual Environment. In this way, dependencies are handled well, conflicts are avoided, and a professional standard for development is set.

The next step is to follow the instructions in Creating Your First Django Project to launch your first project and set the stage for your future robust web app. The project structure and command-line utilities of Django are introduced in this recipe, which is your first practical introduction.

You will learn how to efficiently arrange the components of your project by delving into the modular architecture of Django apps in Exploring the Structure and Purpose of Django Apps. Having this knowledge is essential when developing apps that are both scalable and easy to maintain.

Here in Defining Your Data for Models, we present Django's robust ORM. In this recipe, you will discover the fundamentals of Django modeling and how to use them to construct the data structure of your application based on actual data relationships.

One of the most adored aspects of Django is demonstrated in the Quick Setup and Customization of the Admin Interface. The admin site is a powerful tool for managing your application's data, and you'll learn how to quickly configure it to interact with your models.

The recipe "Simple URL Routing to Views" explains how Django handles requests and returns responses by linking URLs with views. You can't navigate or organize your application without first grasping this basic idea.

In Rendering Data with Templates, you will learn how to use Django's templating engine, which makes it easy to generate HTML text on the fly. You can connect your backend logic with your frontend presentation using this recipe.

At last, Django forms are introduced in Up and Running with Forms and User Input. An important skill for developing interactive web apps is the ability to gather and verify user input.

After finishing this chapter, you will be well-prepared to build simple web applications using Django and take on more advanced tasks.

Recipe 1: Installing Django in a Virtual Environment

Scenario

The first step in beginning to develop with Django is to create a specific workspace for your project. To avoid incompatibilities or conflicts with other Python projects, make sure your development environment is nicely segregated. Installing Django inside a virtual environment is the initial step in this approach.

Desired Solution

Ensure Python is Installed

Before creating a virtual environment, confirm that Python is installed on your system. Django requires Python, and for new projects, the latest version of Python 3 is recommended. If you need to install Python, visit the official Python website for a quick solution:
https://www.python.org/about/gettingstarted/

Verify pip Installation

pip, Python's package manager, is essential for installing Django. It usually comes with Python. If you are unsure whether pip is installed, you can find the installation steps here:
https://pip.pypa.io/en/stable/installing/

Create a Virtual Environment

- Open your terminal or command prompt.
- Navigate to your preferred project directory.
- Execute the following command to create a virtual environment named GitforGits (you may use some other name of your choice):

```
python -m venv gitforgits
```

- This action creates a directory named GitforGits in your project folder, serving as your virtual environment.

Activate the Virtual Environment:

Windows users should activate the environment with:

```
GitforGits\Scripts\activate
```

macOS and Linux users should use:

```
source GitforGits/bin/activate
```

Activation is indicated by the environment's name appearing in the command prompt, signifying that any Python or pip operations now run within this isolated environment.

Install Django

Within the activated virtual environment, install Django by executing:

```
pip install django
```

Verify Django Installation

Confirm Django's successful installation by checking its version:

```
django-admin --version
```

The command returns Django's version, ensuring it is correctly installed and ready for use. Your Django apps will run more smoothly and with less interference if you partition your development environment in this manner.

Recipe 2: Creating Your First Django Project

Scenario

Now that you have installed GitforGits, a virtual environment that is compatible with Django, on your Linux system, you can begin to build your web application. This is a must-do since it lays the groundwork for your project and makes it ready for development. Building the gitforgits project is your first step toward creating a community where coders and those who utilize version control can learn from one another and progress together.

Desired Solution

Activate Your Virtual Environment

Before diving into project creation, ensure you are within the bounds of the **GitforGits** virtual environment. This isolation is key to managing dependencies effectively. If you've stepped out of it, jump back in with:

```
source GitforGits/bin/activate
```

Crafting the New Django Project

With the environment prepped, position yourself in the directory where you envision your project living. Bring your project **gitforgits** into existence with:

```
django-admin startproject gitforgits .
```

The period **.** at the command's tail is deliberate, instructing Django to sprinkle the project's configuration files right into the current directory, helping avoid an extra layer of directory nesting.

Deciphering the Project Structure

Executing the above materializes several files and directories, each playing a unique role in your Django project:

- **manage.py**: A Swiss Army knife for Django, this script facilitates various project interactions.
- **gitforgits/**: This is the core project directory.
- **__init__.py**: A tell-tale file that marks the directory as a Python package.
- **settings.py**: The nerve center of your project, housing configurations.
- **urls.py**: A roadmap of your site's URLs, directing traffic to the correct view.
- **asgi.py** & **wsgi.py**: Gateways for ASGI-compliant and WSGI servers to serve your project, respectively.

Igniting the Development Server

Django arms you with a built-in server tailored for development. Awaken this server and glimpse at your project by running:

```
python manage.py runserver
```

March forth to **http://127.0.0.1:8000/** on your web browser. The appearance of Django's celebratory welcome page signifies a successful project setup. Finishing this recipe has done double duty: it has launched the GitforGits project and shown in simple language how a Django project is structured. You can focus on making your application a reality because every part of the framework you've set up has been carefully crafted to simplify web development.

Recipe 3: Exploring the Structure and Purpose of Django Apps

Scenario

With your Django project **gitforgits** now up and running on your Linux system, it is essential to understand how Django organizes its components. Django projects are collections of apps that work together to accomplish a common goal. To properly modularize your project and make it scalable and manageable, it is crucial to understand the structure and purpose of Django apps. This recipe will walkthrough you through creating your first app within the **gitforgits** project, setting the stage for a well-organized web application.

Desired Solution

Ensure Virtual Environment Activation

Before proceeding, make sure your **GitforGits** virtual environment is active. This encapsulation is crucial for maintaining project integrity. If you've navigated away, re-engage it with:

```
source GitforGits/bin/activate
```

Creating Your First App

Django apps are the building blocks of your project, each responsible for a specific functionality. To create an app named **collaboration**, which will handle user interactions and collaborative features in **gitforgits**, execute:

```
python manage.py startapp collaboration
```

This command constructs a new directory named **collaboration** filled with several files, each serving a specific purpose in the app's lifecycle.

Understanding the App Structure

We shall explore the files and their roles within your newly created **collaboration** app:

- **migrations/**: A directory for database migrations files, managing the evolution of your app's database schema.
- **__init__.py**: Signifies that this directory should be considered a Python package.

- **admin.py**: Where you'll register your models to make them accessible through the Django admin interface.
- **apps.py**: Contains settings for the app itself, such as its name and configuration.
- **models.py**: Defines your app's data models, essentially the structure of your database tables.
- **tests.py**: Reserved for test classes and functions to ensure your app works as expected.
- **views.py**: Houses the views for your app; functions or classes that take a web request and return a web response.

Register the App with Your Project

For Django to acknowledge your app, you must register it within the **gitforgits** project. Open **gitforgits/settings.py** and locate the **INSTALLED_APPS** array. Append your app's name to this list:

```
INSTALLED_APPS = [

...

'collaboration',

]
```

You have learned about the modular architecture that Django promotes and built a new Django app by following this recipe. In order to maintain your Django project organized and flexible, each app should try to encapsulate a cohesive collection of features or behaviors. This is called applying the principle of separation of concerns.

Recipe 4: Defining Your Data for Models

Scenario

Once your Django project is up and running, defining the data models for the GitforGits application is the next crucial step. All Django applications rely on models, which are like a blueprint for your data. They lay out the framework for the database tables and their relationships, which enables the Object-Relational Mapping (ORM) in Django to communicate with the database in a Pythonic manner. One of the most important things for GitforGits is to think of a model that can represent code snippets and user interactions.

Desired Solution

Create an App

Models reside within Django apps. If you haven't already created an app for your code snippets, generate one by executing:

```
python manage.py startapp snippets
```

This command creates a **snippets** directory with the necessary files for a Django app, including a **models.py** file where your models will be defined.

Define the Code Snippet Model

Open the **snippets/models.py** file and define a model to represent a code snippet. Each snippet should have a title, the code content, the language it is written in, and a creation timestamp. Given below is an example:

```
from django.db import models

class Snippet(models.Model):

 title = models.CharField(max_length=100)

 code = models.TextField()

 language = models.CharField(max_length=50)

 created_at = models.DateTimeField(auto_now_add=True)

 def __str__(self):

 return self.title
```

This code defines a **Snippet** model with four fields. The **__str__** method is used to represent each object in the Django admin interface and shell by its title.

Migrate Your Models

After defining your model, you need to create a migration file and apply it to your database to create the corresponding table. Run the following commands:

```
python manage.py makemigrations snippets

python manage.py migrate
```

The **makemigrations** command auto-generates a migration script for the changes you made to your models. The **migrate** command then applies this migration to your database, creating the necessary table(s).

Register Model with Admin Interface

To manage your models easily via Django's built-in admin interface, register the **Snippet** model in **snippets/admin.py**:

```
from django.contrib import admin

from .models import Snippet

admin.site.register(Snippet)
```

Now that you know how to use Django models to encapsulate data structures, you can interface with databases with ease. This is a major step in making your program a reality; with your Snippet model, GitforGits can now process and store code snippets.

Recipe 5: Quick Setup and Customization of Admin Interface

Scenario

To manage your site's content, you can't do better than the Django admin interface. It offers a user-friendly interface for working with database records, including adding, editing, viewing, and removing them. For the GitforGits app, having an easy-to-use admin interface for handling code snippets and user interactions makes administration go more quickly. If you tailor the admin interface to your data models' requirements, you can make content management a breeze.

Desired Solution

Accessing the Admin Site

First, ensure your Django project has an admin superuser created. If you haven't set up a superuser yet, generate one with:

```
python manage.py createsuperuser
```

Follow the prompts to set up the username, email, and password for your superuser. Once created, you can access the admin interface by starting the server (**python manage.py runserver**) and navigating to **http://127.0.0.1:8000/admin/**.

Customizing the Snippet Model Display

To improve how your **Snippet** model appears in the admin interface, you can customize its admin display in the **snippets/admin.py** file where you registered the model. For example, to display more fields in the list view and add a search bar, modify the registration like this:

```
from django.contrib import admin

from .models import Snippet

@admin.register(Snippet)

class SnippetAdmin(admin.ModelAdmin):

 list_display = ('title', 'language', 'created_at')

 list_filter = ('language',)

 search_fields = ('title', 'code')
```

This configuration adds the **language** to the list filter options and enables searching by **title** and **code**.

Customizing Forms in the Admin

For more complex customizations, such as modifying the admin form to include help texts or custom validation, you can define a custom form for your **SnippetAdmin**. Given below is an example:

```
from django import forms

from django.contrib import admin
```

```
from .models import Snippet


class SnippetAdminForm(forms.ModelForm):
 class Meta:
 model = Snippet
 fields = '__all__'
 help_texts = {
 'code': 'Enter your code snippet here.',
 }


@admin.register(Snippet)
class SnippetAdmin(admin.ModelAdmin):
 form = SnippetAdminForm
```

Organizing Fields

You can further organize the form fields in the admin using the **fieldsets** option to group fields into sections. For instance:

```
fieldsets = (
 (None, {
 'fields': ('title', 'language')
 }),
 ('Content', {
```

```
'fields': ('code',),
'description': 'Section for the code snippet itself.'
}),
)
```

By changing the Django admin interface, you can not only make managing content easier, but you can also make the admin page for the GitforGits application easier to use in general. These changes make it easier to find, change, and manage the data that your project is based on. This makes sure that administrative tasks are done as quickly as possible.

Recipe 6: Simple URL Routing to Views

Scenario

Now is the perfect moment to make your data available and interactive on the web. To accomplish this, it is essential to configure URL routing in order to direct web requests to the correct views. The URL is the gateway to the web application in Django; it directs requests to the views that contain the business logic. Our primary goal in developing GitforGits will be to provide a straightforward path that takes people to a page that showcases a collection of code samples.

Desired Solution

Create a View

First, you need to define a view in your app that will be responsible for handling requests to view the list of code snippets. Open or create a **views.py** file within your **snippets** app directory and add the following code:

```
from django.http import HttpResponse
from .models import Snippet
def snippet_list(request):
 """A view to display a list of code snippets."""
 snippets = Snippet.objects.all()
```

```
snippets_list = ', '.join([snippet.title for snippet in snippets])

return HttpResponse(f"List of Snippets: {snippets_list}")
```

This view, **snippet_list**, queries the database for all **Snippet** instances, compiles a list of their titles, and returns an HTTP response containing this list.

Define a URL Pattern

With the view ready, the next step is to map a URL to this view so Django knows which view to invoke when a user requests a specific path. This is done in the **urls.py** file of your main project directory (**gitforgits**). If your project does not already have a dedicated **urls.py** in your app, you'll primarily work with the project's **urls.py** for simplicity.

Open the **gitforgits/urls.py** file and import the **snippet_list** view from your app. Then, add a URL pattern to the **urlpatterns** list:

```
from django.urls import path

from snippets.views import snippet_list

urlpatterns = [

 path('snippets/', snippet_list, name='snippet_list'),

]
```

This pattern tells Django to route any requests with the path **snippets/** to the **snippet_list** view. The **name** parameter is optional but recommended as it allows you to refer to this URL pattern uniquely throughout your project, especially in templates and when using the **reverse** function to dynamically build URLs.

Test Your Route

To see your URL routing in action, make sure your development server is running:

```
python manage.py runserver
```

Then, navigate to **http://127.0.0.1:8000/snippets/** in your web browser. You should see a simple response listing the titles of all code snippets stored in your database, or "List of Snippets:" if none are present.

Users are able to access and interact with the data maintained by your Django models using this arrangement, which forms the backbone of your application's web interface.

Recipe 7: Rendering Data with Templates

Scenario

Now that we have the data, we shall try to improve the user experience by using templates to display it. Dynamic HTML generation is made possible via Django's templating system, which provides a more organized and styled way to display data. Using templates, we will not only provide plain text responses but also generate an HTML page that displays all code snippets in a more organized and user-friendly manner.

Desired Solution

Create a Template

First, you need a template file where you'll define the HTML structure for displaying your code snippets. Within your **snippets** app, create a directory named **templates**, and inside it, another directory named **snippets** to prevent template naming conflicts between apps. Then, create a file named **snippet_list.html** within this directory:

```
snippets/

└── templates/

 └── snippets/

 └── snippet_list.html
```

Inside **snippet_list.html**, add the following HTML code:

```
<!DOCTYPE html>

<html lang="en">

<head>

 <meta charset="UTF-8">
```

```
<title>Snippet List</title>

</head>

<body>

<h1>List of Snippets</h1>

<ul>

{% for snippet in snippets %}

<li>{{ snippet.title }}: {{ snippet.code }}</li>

{% empty %}

<li>No snippets found.</li>

{% endfor %}

</ul>

</body>

</html>
```

This template uses Django's template language to iterate over the **snippets** context variable, expected to be a list of **Snippet** instances, displaying each snippet's title and code.

Update the View to Use the Template

Modify the **snippet_list** view in your **snippets/views.py** file to render the **snippet_list.html** template:

```
from django.shortcuts import render

from .models import Snippet

def snippet_list(request):

 snippets = Snippet.objects.all()
```

```
return render(request, 'snippets/snippet_list.html', {'snippets': snippets})
```

The **render** function takes the request object, the path to the template, and a context dictionary as arguments. It renders the template with the provided context, generating a dynamic HTML page as the response.

Test Your Template

Ensure your development server is running, and navigate to **http://127.0.0.1:8000/snippets/** in your web browser. You should now see a styled HTML page listing the titles and code of all snippets in your database, or a message indicating no snippets are found.

To improve the user experience of your Django apps, you may efficiently build complex web pages by defining HTML structures in templates and dynamically populating them with data from your views.

Recipe 8: Up and Running with Forms and User Input

Scenario

To encourage participation and teamwork in the GitforGits project, it is crucial to accept user-submitted code snippets. The robust forms framework in Django makes form handling easy by allowing the display and processing of forms with little code. In this recipe, you will learn all you need to know to build a code snippet submission form, from using a template to securely processing user input to presenting the form.

Desired Solution

Define a Form

Within the **snippets** app, create a file named **forms.py** to define your form classes. Add the following code to create a form for the **Snippet** model:

```
from django import forms

from .models import Snippet
```

```
class SnippetForm(forms.ModelForm):

 class Meta:

 model = Snippet

 fields = ['title', 'code', 'language']
```

This **SnippetForm** class automatically generates a form with fields corresponding to the **Snippet** model attributes you specify in the **fields** list.

Create a View for Form Submission

In **snippets/views.py**, add a new view to handle the display and processing of the **SnippetForm**:

```
from django.shortcuts import render, redirect

from .forms import SnippetForm

def submit_snippet(request):

 if request.method == 'POST':

 form = SnippetForm(request.POST)

 if form.is_valid():

 form.save()

 return redirect('snippet_list')

 else:

 form = SnippetForm()

 return render(request, 'snippets/submit_snippet.html', {'form': form})
```

This view handles both GET requests (displaying the form) and POST requests (processing form submissions). If the form is valid upon submission, it saves the new snippet to the database and redirects the user to the snippet list page.

Create a Template for the Form

In the **snippets/templates/snippets** directory, create a new template named **submit_snippet.html** for rendering the form:

```
<!DOCTYPE html>
<html lang="en">
<head>
 <meta charset="UTF-8">
 <title>Submit Snippet</title>
</head>
<body>
 <h1>Submit a New Snippet</h1>
 <form method="post">
 {% csrf_token %}
 {{ form.as_p }}
 <button type="submit">Submit</button>
 </form>
</body>
</html>
```

This template includes a CSRF token for security, renders the form as paragraph elements (**as_p**), and provides a submit button.

Update URLconf for the Form View

In **gitforgits/urls.py**, import the **submit_snippet** view and add a new URL pattern:

```
from snippets.views import snippet_list, submit_snippet

urlpatterns = [

 path('snippets/', snippet_list, name='snippet_list'),

 path('submit/', submit_snippet, name='submit_snippet'),

]
```

Test Form Submission

With your development server running, navigate to **http://127.0.0.1:8000/submit/** in your web browser. You should see the form for submitting new snippets. Try adding a snippet to ensure it is saved to the database and that you are redirected to the list of snippets upon successful submission. This functionality is key to building interactive and dynamic web applications.

Summary

In this chapter, we began the basics of Django development by creating a clean, isolated development environment with Django deployed in a virtual environment called GitforGit. This initial step guaranteed that our project's dependencies were properly managed and did not conflict with other Python projects. We next created our first Django project, gitforgits, learning about the structure and function of Django apps, which serve as the foundation of our web application. This included a deep dive into constructing data models, where we learnt how to create a Snippet model to represent code snippets and how to use Django's strong ORM system to interface with the database in Python.

The learnings proceeded with the modification of the Django admin interface, which demonstrated Django's rapid development capabilities by allowing us to quickly create an interface for maintaining our models. This demonstrated Django's "batteries-included" attitude by providing us with a complete set of tools for standard web development activities. Following that, we implemented simple URL routing to connect web requests to the right views, which was a critical step in making our application accessible via the web. We then experimented with Django's templating mechanism to render data in dynamic HTML, allowing for a better presentation of our data. This was critical for developing compelling user interfaces and optimizing the overall user experience.

The conclusion of Chapter 1's learning led us to managing forms and user input, where we learned about Django's forms system. This enabled us to collect user input in a secure and fast manner, increasing the interactivity of our web application. Throughout this chapter, the step-by-step method to developing a Django application from the ground up not only built a solid basis for our project, GitforGits, but also provided us with the knowledge and skills to handle more complicated web development challenges. Each recipe provides a unique learning experience by stressing practical application and avoiding repetition, smoothly building on prior lessons to encourage a thorough understanding of Django's basic features.

CHAPTER 2: DEEP DIVE INTO MODELS AND DATABASES

Introduction

This chapter takes you from an introduction to Django project setup to an in-depth look at the Object-Relational Mapping (ORM) system and all its features. This chapter is carefully crafted to deepen our technical ability of Django's database interactions, so we can model complex data relationships, improve the functionality of our models, and optimize the performance of our database queries. You will be prepared to take on complex database design and manipulation tasks in their own Django projects as we explore real-world scenarios that reflect the complexities of models and databases.

In the first part of the chapter, "Handling Complex Model Relationships," we will learn how to use Django to create and manage relationships between many objects, individuals, and several entities. This includes learning how to improve the relational component of our database design by structuring models to reflect actual relationships between various entities. After this, we will customize our database queries to retrieve data more efficiently and intuitively by exploring Working with Custom Managers and QuerySets. Making our codebase more readable and maintainable will involve crafting custom methods to encapsulate common query patterns.

An important portion of this chapter will be devoted to the topic of using Django Signals for Model Changes. This feature is useful because it lets developers execute custom logic at different points in the model lifecycle, like when the model is being created or updated. Additionally, we will learn how to implement soft deletion in models, which is a method that preserves data integrity and allows for data recovery by marking records as deleted without actually removing them from the database.

With that being said, we will explore methods to keep our database consistent and dependable as it grows. Methods for field validation and transaction management are part of this. After that, we go beyond Django's built-in object relationship management (ORM) capabilities by integrating with external databases. This section shows us how to link our Django project to various database systems, so we can build more advanced applications.

Lastly, we will cover performance in Implementing Index and Query Optimization. This will teach us how to optimize our database queries and structure for speed and efficiency, which is a crucial skill for creating web applications with high performance. You will gain a thorough understanding of Django's model and database capabilities through this chapter's practical examples and detailed explanations. This will set the stage for developing web applications that are robust, scalable, and efficient.

Recipe 1: Handling Complex Model Relationships

Scenario

In order to build complex web applications, it is common to need to model complex relationships between various data sets. You can make your app reflect real-world complexities with the help of Django's ORM, which offers powerful tools for defining these relationships. To build a social network, an e-commerce platform, or an application like GitforGits, you need to know how to implement OneToOne, ForeignKey, ManyToMany, and GenericForeignKey relationships. There is a specific use for each type; for example, user profiles associated with accounts and code snippets can be classified using tags.

Desired Solution

OneToOneField Relationship

Used to create a one-to-one link between two models, where one record in a model corresponds to one record in another model. This is ideal for extending existing models. For example, extending the User model with user profile information:

```
from django.conf import settings

from django.db import models

class UserProfile(models.Model):

 user = models.OneToOneField(settings.AUTH_USER_MODEL,
on_delete=models.CASCADE)

 bio = models.TextField()
```

ForeignKey Relationship

A ForeignKey defines a many-to-one relationship, meaning a model can belong to another model on a "many" side of the relationship. This is useful for scenarios like assigning multiple code snippets to a single user:

```
class Snippet(models.Model):

 author = models.ForeignKey(settings.AUTH_USER_MODEL,
on_delete=models.CASCADE, related_name='snippets')

 title = models.CharField(max_length=100)

 code = models.TextField()
```

ManyToManyField Relationship

For relationships where an instance of one model can be associated with many instances of another model, and vice versa. A typical use case is tagging code snippets where both tags and snippets can have multiple associations:

```
class Tag(models.Model):

 name = models.CharField(max_length=30)

 snippets = models.ManyToManyField(Snippet, related_name='tags')
```

GenericForeignKey Relationship

Used for cases where a model can relate to multiple other models. Django's contenttypes framework facilitates this. It is slightly more complex but invaluable for situations like comments, where a single comment model can associate with any model:

```
from django.contrib.contenttypes.fields import GenericForeignKey

from django.contrib.contenttypes.models import ContentType

from django.db import models

class Comment(models.Model):

 content_type = models.ForeignKey(ContentType, on_delete=models.CASCADE)

 object_id = models.PositiveIntegerField()

 content_object = GenericForeignKey('content_type', 'object_id')

 text = models.TextField()
```

Note: Working with **GenericForeignKey** requires a good understanding of Django's **ContentType** framework and is used when your application requires a flexible association between models.

After defining these relationships, it is crucial to create and run migrations to apply the changes to your database schema. Then, you can start creating instances of your models in the Django shell or admin to test the relationships. Django's ORM tools like **select_related**, **prefetch_related**, and query filtering across related objects will help you efficiently query these complex relationships. This recipe provides an introduction to Django's relational fields, which are essential for learning more complex data modeling techniques.

Recipe 2: Working with Custom Managers and QuerySets

Scenario

Once we've explored the various types of relationships that models can have in Django, improving our database interactions with these models becomes critical for efficient and clean code. Although Django's ORM is very powerful, there are instances when you may desire additional control or a way to simplify frequent queries on your models. Here, QuerySets and custom managers become useful. A more natural way to retrieve data and less code duplication are both achieved by extending Django's querying capabilities with methods that are specific to your needs. To improve the interaction with the models we defined earlier, this recipe will lead you through the creation of custom managers and QuerySets.

Desired Solution

Understand the Default Manager

Django models come with a default manager named **objects**. It is the gateway to Django's database query operations. While powerful, the default manager might not cater to all your specific querying needs.

Define a Custom QuerySet

For this recipe, we shall assume we're working with a **Snippet** model from a previous recipe. You often need to query snippets that are marked as 'featured' or perform a complex query to retrieve snippets based on language and length. Start by defining a custom QuerySet in your **models.py**:

```
from django.db import models

class SnippetQuerySet(models.QuerySet):

 def featured(self):

 return self.filter(is_featured=True)

 def by_language(self, language):
```

```
return self.filter(language=language)

def short_snippets(self, max_length=100):

return self.filter(length__lte=max_length)
```

This custom QuerySet, **SnippetQuerySet**, provides three methods: **featured()**, **by_language()**, and **short_snippets()**, each encapsulating a specific query.

Create a Custom Manager

Let us now integrate this **SnippetQuerySet** with a custom manager to make these methods accessible through the manager:

```
class SnippetManager(models.Manager):

def get_queryset(self):

return SnippetQuerySet(self.model, using=self._db)

def featured(self):

return self.get_queryset().featured()

def by_language(self, language):

return self.get_queryset().by_language(language)

def short_snippets(self, max_length=100):

return self.get_queryset().short_snippets(max_length)
```

In this case, **SnippetManager** overrides the **get_queryset()** method to return instances of our custom QuerySet. It also provides convenience methods to directly access the custom QuerySet methods.

Attach the Custom Manager to Your Model

Finally, apply this custom manager to your **Snippet** model:

```
class Snippet(models.Model):
```

```
# model fields go here

objects = SnippetManager()
```

By assigning **SnippetManager()** to the **objects** attribute, you replace the default manager with your custom one, making the custom QuerySet methods accessible through **Snippet.objects**.

With the custom manager and QuerySets set up, you can now easily retrieve model instances using the defined methods, simplifying your code and making your model interactions more expressive. For instance, to get all featured snippets, you can use **Snippet.objects.featured()**. This approach not only enhances code readability but also centralizes query logic within the model layer, adhering to Django's DRY (Don't Repeat Yourself) principle.

Recipe 3: Utilizing Django Signals for Model Changes

Scenario

In some cases, you'll need to react to changes in your models by taking specific measures. For example, you may wish to record actions, notify users, or update relevant data whenever a model is saved or removed. Django signals are a great way to decouple actions that need to happen in response to certain actions because they let you listen for and respond to specific framework events, like model changes.

Desired Solution

Understanding Signals

Django includes a set of built-in signals that send notifications when certain actions occur. The most commonly used signals are **pre_save**, **post_save**, **pre_delete**, and **post_delete**, which are dispatched before or after a model's **save** and **delete** methods are called, respectively.

Creating Signal Handlers

A signal handler is a function that gets executed in response to a signal. For example, to create a signal handler that logs when a new **Snippet** is created, you can define the following function:

```
from django.db.models.signals import post_save

from django.dispatch import receiver
```

```
from .models import Snippet

@receiver(post_save, sender=Snippet)

def snippet_created(sender, instance, created, **kwargs):

 if created:

 print(f"New snippet created: {instance.title}")
```

This handler listens for the **post_save** signal from the **Snippet** model. When a new snippet is saved, it checks if the **created** argument is **True**, indicating a new record has been created, and prints a message to the console.

Registering Signal Handlers

The **@receiver** decorator is used to register the signal handler. The first argument specifies the signal you are listening for, and the **sender** argument specifies the model class sending the signal. This setup ensures that **snippet_created** is called every time a new **Snippet** instance is saved.

Using Signals for Complex Operations

Signals can be used for more complex operations beyond logging, such as automatically creating related records, sending emails, or invalidating caches. The power of signals lies in their ability to execute additional logic in response to changes in your database, all while keeping your models' code clean and focused on their primary responsibilities.

Recipe 4: Implementing Soft Deletion in Models

Scenario

There may be times when you should not remove records from the database irretrievably. You would rather mark them as deleted so the data remains intact for future use in analysis, recovery, or record-keeping. Applications where data permanence is crucial can benefit significantly from this concept, which is called soft deletion. With Django's soft deletion feature, you can hide "deleted" records from regular queries but still access them when needed. This requires a different way of thinking about model definition and querying.

Desired Solution

Extending the Model to Support Soft Deletion

To implement soft deletion, you can add a **is_deleted** field to your models, indicating whether a record is considered deleted. For the **Snippet** model, the modification would look like this:

```
from django.db import models

class Snippet(models.Model):

 title = models.CharField(max_length=100)

 code = models.TextField()

 language = models.CharField(max_length=50)

 created_at = models.DateTimeField(auto_now_add=True)

 is_deleted = models.BooleanField(default=False)

 def delete(self, *args, **kwargs):

 self.is_deleted = True

 self.save()

 def __str__(self):

 return self.title
```

In this case, the **delete** method is overridden to set the **is_deleted** flag to **True** instead of actually deleting the record from the database.

Customizing Manager to Exclude Soft Deleted Records

To ensure that soft-deleted records are not included in query results by default, you can define a custom manager for the model:

```
class SnippetManager(models.Manager):

 def get_queryset(self):

 return super().get_queryset().filter(is_deleted=False)
```

```
class Snippet(models.Model):

 # Model fields as defined previously...

 objects = SnippetManager()
```

This custom manager overrides the **get_queryset** method to filter out records where **is_deleted** is **True**.

Retrieving Soft Deleted Records

If you need to access soft-deleted records (for example, in an admin interface or for data recovery purposes), you can add another manager that includes these records:

```
class AllSnippetsManager(models.Manager):

 def get_queryset(self):

 return super().get_queryset()

class Snippet(models.Model):

 # Model fields and the default manager as defined previously...

 all_objects = AllSnippetsManager()
```

With this setup, **Snippet.objects.all()** will return only non-deleted records, while **Snippet.all_objects.all()** will include both deleted and non-deleted records.

There is no permanent removal of records from your database when you use soft deletion, which gives you more control over your data. Applications requiring data recovery or the preservation of historical data integrity may find this approach to be of utmost value. In addition to showing you how to implement soft deletion in Django models, this recipe also illustrates how flexible Django's ORM is, so you can modify data handling to fit your application's needs.

Recipe 5: Maintaining Data Integrity

Scenario

Ensuring data integrity is all about keeping data accurate, consistent, and reliable at all times.

Multiple mechanisms in Django, such as model constraints, transaction management, and careful handling of model relationships, allow for this to be accomplished. This recipe delves into methods for keeping data intact, guaranteeing that the GitforGits application stays strong, precise, and reliable.

Desired Solution

Using Model Field Options

Django models offer a variety of field options that can be used to enforce data integrity at the database level. For instance, the **unique** attribute ensures that no two records in a table have the same value for a specific field. Additionally, **null** and **blank** can control whether a field can be empty, and **choices** limit the values that a field can accept.

```
class Snippet(models.Model):
 LANGUAGE_CHOICES = [
 ('PY', 'Python'),
 ('JS', 'JavaScript'),
 ('HTML', 'HTML'),
 ]
 title = models.CharField(max_length=100, unique=True)
 language = models.CharField(max_length=50, choices=LANGUAGE_CHOICES)
```

These constraints are enforced by Django at the model level and by the database, ensuring data consistency.

Implementing Custom Validators

For more complex validation rules that cannot be enforced through model field options, Django allows you to define custom validators. These can be applied at the field level or as model clean methods.

```
from django.core.exceptions import ValidationError
def validate_code(value):
```

```
if "import" in value:

raise ValidationError("Code cannot contain import statements.")

class Snippet(models.Model):

code = models.TextField(validators=[validate_code])
```

This validator prevents users from including import statements in their code snippets, a simple rule to enhance security.

Utilizing Django's Transaction Management

Transactions ensure that a series of database operations either all succeed or fail together, maintaining data consistency especially in complex operations involving multiple steps.

```
from django.db import transaction

def create_snippet_with_tags(title, code, tags):

with transaction.atomic():

snippet = Snippet.objects.create(title=title, code=code)

for tag in tags:

snippet.tags.add(tag)
```

Here, the creation of a snippet and its associated tags is atomic, ensuring that either all operations succeed or none at all, preserving database integrity.

Overriding Save and Delete Methods

For additional control over data integrity, you can override the **save** and **delete** methods of a model. This is useful for implementing custom logic before saving or deleting an object, such as validation checks or cleanup of related data.

```
class Snippet(models.Model):

# Model fields as defined previously...
```

```
def save(self, *args, **kwargs):
# Custom logic before saving...
super().save(*args, **kwargs)
# Custom logic after saving...
```

You can keep your application's data consistent, accurate, and secure by using Django's data constraints, input validation, transaction management, and model behavior customization.

Recipe 6: Integrating with External Databases (PostgreSQL)

Scenario

Although SQLite is Django's default database, PostgreSQL or a non-relational database like MongoDB are usually more suitable for real-world applications due to their robustness and scalability. The application's capabilities are enhanced by integrating Django with these external databases. This results in improved performance, scalability, and a broader set of features that are suitable for complex projects. This recipe will center on the integration of Django with PostgreSQL.

Desired Solution

Install PostgreSQL

First, ensure that PostgreSQL is installed on your system. You can download it from the **official PostgreSQL website** or use a package manager on Linux. After installation, create a database for your Django project.

Install psycopg2

Django uses the **psycopg2** package as the PostgreSQL database adapter. Install it in your **GitforGits** virtual environment by running:

```
pip install psycopg2
```

Configure Django to Use PostgreSQL

Modify your Django project's settings file (**gitforgits/settings.py**) to configure the **DATABASES** setting to use PostgreSQL:

```
DATABASES = {
 'default': {
 'ENGINE': 'django.db.backends.postgresql',
 'NAME': 'gitforgitsdb',
 'USER': 'your_postgresql_username',
 'PASSWORD': 'your_password',
 'HOST': 'localhost',
 'PORT': '', # Leave as an empty string to use the default port.
 }
}
```

Replace **'your_postgresql_username'** and **'your_password'** with your actual PostgreSQL username and password. The **'NAME'** is the name of the database you created for your Django project.

Migrate Django Models to PostgreSQL

With the database settings configured, run Django's migrate command to create your model tables in the PostgreSQL database:

```
python manage.py migrate
```

This command examines your **INSTALLED_APPS** setting and creates the necessary database tables according to the database configurations specified in your **DATABASES** setting and the models defined in your applications.

Verify the Connection

Run your Django development server:

```
Python

manage.py runserver
```

Then, use Django's admin or shell to create or query objects. This ensures that Django can successfully communicate with the PostgreSQL database. This setup is ideal for applications like GitforGits, expected to scale and handle complex data operations.

Recipe 7: Implementing Index and Query Optimization

Scenario

When your Django application experiences a surge in data volume and user base, it is essential to optimize your database queries to ensure consistent performance. Users may become frustrated when their application experience is sluggish due to slow queries. With Django, you can optimize database queries and implement indexing strategies to make your data retrieval times much faster. This will make your application run smoothly and efficiently.

Desired Solution

Understanding the Need for Indexes

Indexes are used by databases to quickly locate data without having to search every row in a table every time a database table is accessed. Indexes can be particularly beneficial for columns that are frequently queried or used as part of a **JOIN** operation in your SQL queries.

Adding Indexes to Models

To add an index to a model field in Django, you can use the **db_index** parameter. For example, if we identify that the **title** field of the **Snippet** model is often queried, we can optimize it like so:

```
class Snippet(models.Model):

 title = models.CharField(max_length=100, db_index=True)

 # Other fields remain unchanged
```

This will create a database index for the **title** field, improving the performance of queries filtering or ordering by this field.

Using Meta Options for Compound Indexes

Sometimes, you may need to create indexes that span multiple fields, known as compound indexes. This can be done in Django by defining a **Meta** class inside your model class and specifying the **indexes** option:

```
class Snippet(models.Model):

 # Model fields...

  class Meta:

 indexes = [

 models.Index(fields=['title', 'language']),

 ]
```

This creates a compound index on the **title** and **language** fields, which can speed up queries that filter or sort based on these two fields together.

Optimizing Queries with select_related and prefetch_related

Django's ORM allows you to optimize your queries further by reducing the number of database hits. For ForeignKey relationships, **select_related** can be used to perform a SQL join and fetch related objects in a single query. Meanwhile, **prefetch_related** is used for ManyToMany and reverse ForeignKey relationships, fetching related objects in a separate query and joining them in Python, which can be more efficient than multiple database hits.

```
snippets = Snippet.objects.select_related('user').all() # Assuming a 'user' ForeignKey

snippets = Snippet.objects.prefetch_related('tags').all() # Assuming a 'tags'
ManyToManyField
```

Keep an eye on your queries' performance using Django's built-in logging or by using the **django-debug-toolbar** package. It provides detailed information about queries including execution time, allowing you to identify bottlenecks. And, you should review and optimize your database queries regularly as part of app development.

Summary

The strong capabilities of Django's object relationship management (ORM) for managing complicated data structures, improving model functionality, and optimizing database interactions were the focus of this chapter, which advanced our exploration of Django. We started by delving into the complexities of handling complex model relationships, such as OneToOne, ForeignKey, and ManyToMany fields. With this groundwork, we were able to improve the relational dynamics of our application's data model by organizing and relating data within our database.

The chapter took us further into the topic, custom managers and querysets, which allowed us to simplify data access and manipulation using custom methods and encapsulate common query patterns. Our codebase became more maintainable and our application became more efficient as a result of this. We continued our learning by looking at Django signals for model changes, a robust feature that allows us to respond to events in the ORM lifecycle with actions like sending notifications when data changes or automatically updating related fields. In addition, we learned soft deletion, a method that allows users to mark records as deleted without actually deleting them from the database. This way, we can keep the data for future reference or analysis while still controlling who can access it.

This chapter also made us realize how important it is to keep data integrity using different methods, such as field options, custom validators, and transaction management, to make sure that the data in our application is reliable and consistent. We also explored the possibility of connecting Django to third-party databases, such as PostgreSQL. At last, the chapter covered index and query optimization, which taught us how to use Django's ORM tools and database indexing to make our web app faster.

CHAPTER 3: MASTERING DJANGO'S URL DISPATCHER AND VIEWS

Introduction

In this chapter, we will move our attention to the most important part of using Django for web development: making an intuitive and responsive web app through efficient management of URLs and views. To help developers create projects like GitforGits with logical structure and smooth navigation, this chapter explores the internals of Django's URL dispatcher and the smart use of class-based and function-based views. This chapter's goal is to teach you how to build dynamic, user-friendly web applications by breaking down different scenarios and providing them with the knowledge to implement advanced URL routing strategies.

Beginning with the Implementing Dynamic URL Routing technique, we will jump into the process of creating dynamic URLs that can adjust to a web application's changing requirements, making it more scalable and easier to maintain. One important method for making dynamic web pages is to use path converters to extract values from URLs and then inject them into views. After this, we will go over how to use namespaces to keep your project's URL structure organized and scalable, how to use advanced URL configurations to keep your apps' URLs clear, and how to handle conflicts that may arise.

We will go over two separate methods for dealing with form data: one using class-based views and the other using function-based views. This is because form data handling is fundamental to web applications. To give developers greater freedom in how they incorporate user input and interaction mechanisms, each recipe will show the benefits of class-based views compared to function-based views in form management. This recipe shows you how to use Django's built-in generic views for common web development patterns, which cuts down on the amount of code needed to do things like showing a list of objects or processing form submissions.

Two other recipes that will help web apps be more secure and robust are one on creating custom middleware for request processing and the other on securing views with permissions and user checks. The first recipe will teach you how to process requests, and the second will teach you how to protect views from unauthorized access. A combination of view-level permissions and custom request processing and response modification implemented by middleware allows developers to restrict access to certain areas of an application to authorized users only. With the help of the detailed recipes provided in this chapter, developers will be able to use Django's URL dispatcher and views more effectively, allowing them to create robust yet user-friendly web applications.

Recipe 1: Implement Dynamic URL Routing Technique

Scenario

Web application developers rely on dynamic URL routing, which lets them make efficient and adaptable URL patterns based on the content being delivered. If you want to build scalable and maintainable apps in Django, you need to learn dynamic URL routing. With dynamic routing, the application can manage a diverse set of web pages in a unified manner, whether they are displaying user profiles, blog posts, or product details. Without having to create unique URL patterns for each feature, GitforGits will be able to display individual code snippets or user profiles with the help of dynamic URL routing.

Desired Solution

Defining Dynamic URL Patterns

In Django, dynamic URL patterns are defined using path converters in your **urls.py** file. These converters specify the type of variable you expect to capture from the URL. For example, to create a dynamic route for viewing individual snippets by their ID, update the **urls.py** within your **snippets** app:

```
from django.urls import path

from . import views

urlpatterns = [

 path('snippets/<int:id>/', views.snippet_detail, name='snippet_detail'),

]
```

In this case, **<int:id>** is a path converter that captures an integer value from the URL and passes it as an **id** argument to the **snippet_detail** view function.

Creating the View Function

In **views.py** of your **snippets** app, define the **snippet_detail** view to handle requests for individual snippets:

```
from django.http import HttpResponse

from .models import Snippet

def snippet_detail(request, id):

 try:

 snippet = Snippet.objects.get(id=id)
```

```
return HttpResponse(f"Viewing snippet: {snippet.title}")

except Snippet.DoesNotExist:

return HttpResponse("Snippet not found.", status=404)
```

This function attempts to retrieve a **Snippet** instance by its **id**. If found, it responds with the snippet's title; otherwise, it returns a 404 response.

Testing the Dynamic Route

With the dynamic URL pattern and view in place, start the Django development server (if it is not already running) and navigate to **/snippets/1/** (assuming a snippet with ID 1 exists) in your web browser. You should see a response displaying the title of the snippet with ID 1. This recipe introduces the concept and implementation of dynamic URL routing in Django and with leveraging the path converters, you can efficiently design your URL patterns to handle a wide variety of content with minimal configuration.

Recipe 2: Using Advanced URL Configurations and Namespacing

Scenario

It is becoming more and more difficult to incorporate numerous apps and manage URL configurations. When things aren't organized well, URL pattern collisions and naming confusion are more likely to occur. Critical Django techniques like namespacing and advanced URL configurations help with these problems by giving a structured way to organize URL patterns and make sure they are unique throughout the project. In addition to improving maintainability, this method makes reversing URLs in templates and views much easier.

Desired Solution

Organizing URLs with Include

Django’s **include()** function allows you to reference URL configurations from different apps within the main project’s **urls.py**. This modular approach keeps URL configurations clean and app-focused. For instance, if your project has a **snippets** app, you can include its URLs like this in your project’s **gitforgits/urls.py**:

```
from django.urls import path, include
```

```
urlpatterns = [
 path('snippets/', include('snippets.urls')),
]
```

This means any URL path that starts with **snippets/** will use the URL patterns defined in **snippets/urls.py**, allowing app-specific URL configurations.

Applying Namespacing to Apps

To avoid naming collisions and to simplify URL name referencing, you can apply namespacing to your app's URLs. In your app's **urls.py** (e.g., **snippets/urls.py**), add an **app_name** variable that defines the namespace:

```
from django.urls import path
from . import views
app_name = 'snippets'
urlpatterns = [
 path('<int:id>/', views.snippet_detail, name='snippet_detail'),
]
```

You can now reverse URLs with namespacing, ensuring that URL names are unique across your project. For instance, to reverse the **snippet_detail** URL in a template, you would use:

```
{% url 'snippets:snippet_detail' id=snippet.id %}
```

Reversing Namespaced URLs in Views

Namespaced URLs can also be reversed in views using Django's **reverse** function, facilitating dynamic URL creation:

```
from django.urls import reverse
```

```
def my_view(request):

 detail_url = reverse('snippets:snippet_detail', kwargs={'id': 1})

 # Use detail_url as needed...
```

This approach is particularly useful for redirecting users or constructing links dynamically within your views, ensuring that the references remain valid even if the URL patterns change. This setup not only prevents potential conflicts as your application scales but also makes URL management more intuitive, supporting a cleaner codebase and more reliable URL referencing throughout your application.

Recipe 3: Handling Form Data with Class-Based Views

Scenario

The effectiveness of interactive user experiences relies on the efficient handling of forms. By encapsulating common patterns like displaying and processing forms into class methods, Django's class-based views (CBVs) provide a structured, reusable approach to handling form submissions. This method streamlines the execution of form logic while simultaneously encouraging code reusability and maintainability. Making use of CBVs can simplify operations like adding or modifying code snippets for GitforGits, which in turn makes the application more scalable and modular.

Desired Solution

Creating a Form

First, define a Django form for your model. Assuming we have a **Snippet** model and you want to create a form to add or edit snippets, define a **SnippetForm** in your **forms.py** within the **snippets** app:

```
from django import forms

from .models import Snippet

class SnippetForm(forms.ModelForm):
```

```
class Meta:
model = Snippet
fields = ['title', 'code', 'language']
```

This form class automatically generates fields for the **Snippet** model's attributes.

Implementing a Class-Based View

With the form defined, implement a CBV in **views.py** that handles both displaying and processing the form. Django's **FormView** is a convenient base class for form views:

```
from django.urls import reverse_lazy
from django.views.generic.edit import FormView
from .forms import SnippetForm
class SnippetCreateView(FormView):
template_name = 'snippets/snippet_form.html'
form_class = SnippetForm
success_url = reverse_lazy('snippets:snippet_list')
def form_valid(self, form):
# This method is called when valid form data has been POSTed.
# It should return an HttpResponse.
form.save()
return super().form_valid(form)
```

In this view, **template_name** specifies the template used to render the form, **form_class** denotes the form to be handled, and **success_url** is where the user will be redirected upon successful form submission. The **form_valid** method is overridden to save the form when valid data is submitted.

Configuring the URL

Link the CBV to a URL in **snippets/urls.py** by adding an entry to the **urlpatterns** list:

```
from django.urls import path

from .views import SnippetCreateView

urlpatterns = [

 path('create/', SnippetCreateView.as_view(), name='snippet_create'),

]
```

This makes the form accessible at the path **/snippets/create/**, where users can add new snippets.

Creating the Form Template

Finally, create a template named **snippet_form.html** in the **snippets/templates/snippets/** directory. The template should render the form and handle submission:

```
<h2>Add New Snippet</h2>

<form method="post">

 {% csrf_token %}

 {{ form.as_p }}

 <button type="submit">Submit</button>

</form>
```

This template displays the form fields and a submit button, using **POST** method for form submission.This approach not only simplifies the code but also enhances the maintainability and scalability of the application with the **SnippetCreateView**.

Recipe 4: Handling Form Data with Function-

Based Views

Scenario

For simple form processing tasks in particular, function-based views (FBVs) offer simplicity and flexibility, in contrast to Django's class-based views, which offer a structured approach to form handling. For our application, FBVs are a lifesaver when it comes to implementing forms for user submissions or data entry quickly and easily, all without the hassle of class-based views. For developers who like to take a more hands-on approach to processing requests, they are significant because they allow for direct, procedural handling.

Desired Solution

Defining a Form

Assuming the existence of a **Snippet** model, you first need to define a form in **forms.py** within the **snippets** app, similar to what was done for class-based views:

```
from django import forms

from .models import Snippet

class SnippetForm(forms.ModelForm):

 class Meta:

 model = Snippet

 fields = ['title', 'code', 'language']
```

This **SnippetForm** will be used to capture user input for creating or editing snippets.

Creating the Function-Based View

In your **views.py** file, create a function to handle both GET and POST requests for the form:

```
from django.shortcuts import render, redirect

from .forms import SnippetForm

def create_snippet(request):
```

```
if request.method == 'POST':
form = SnippetForm(request.POST)
if form.is_valid():
form.save()
return redirect('snippets:snippet_list')
else:
form = SnippetForm()
return render(request, 'snippets/snippet_form.html', {'form': form})
```

This view function checks the request method. If it is a POST request, it attempts to save the form with submitted data; if the form is valid, it redirects the user to the snippet listing page. For GET requests, it displays an empty form.

Configuring the URL

Connect your FBV to a URL in **snippets/urls.py**:

```
from django.urls import path
from .views import create_snippet
urlpatterns = [
path('create/', create_snippet, name='snippet_create'),
]
```

This step makes the form accessible through the specified path, integrating it into the Django app's URL configurations.

Creating the Form Template

The form template **snippet_form.html** in **snippets/templates/snippets/** directory can be identical to the one used for class-based views:

```
<h2>Add New Snippet</h2>
<form method="post">
 {% csrf_token %}
 {{ form.as_p }}
 <button type="submit">Submit</button>
</form>
```

This ensures users have a consistent experience, regardless of the backend view handling the form.

Recipe 5: Leveraging Django's Generic Views

Scenario

Web development tasks like showing a list of objects or handling form submissions are made easier with Django's generic views, which abstract common patterns into simple, reusable classes. For our application, where code reuse and efficiency are key, using generic views can drastically cut down on the amount of code needed for common web functions like listing or creating code snippets. Here we will look at how to use Django's generic views to build these popular web patterns with less code, which will make development faster and easier to maintain.

Desired Solution

Using ListView for Displaying Objects

Suppose you want to display a list of all code snippets. Instead of writing a view from scratch, you can use Django's **ListView**. In **views.py** of your **snippets** app, import **ListView** and create a subclass to display all **Snippet** objects:

```
from django.views.generic import ListView
from .models import Snippet
class SnippetListView(ListView):
 model = Snippet
```

```
    template_name = 'snippets/snippet_list.html'

    context_object_name = 'snippets'
```

This view automatically queries the database for all **Snippet** objects and passes them to the **snippet_list.html** template under the context variable **snippets**.

Using CreateView for Form Handling

For creating new snippets, Django's **CreateView** simplifies the process. It handles form display, validation, and saving the object upon form submission. Define a **CreateView** for the **Snippet** model:

```
from django.views.generic.edit import CreateView

from django.urls import reverse_lazy

from .models import Snippet

from .forms import SnippetForm

class SnippetCreateView(CreateView):

    model = Snippet

    form_class = SnippetForm

    template_name = 'snippets/snippet_form.html'

    success_url = reverse_lazy('snippets:snippet_list')
```

This view uses the **SnippetForm**, renders the **snippet_form.html** template for form display, and redirects to the snippet list view upon successful form submission.

Configuring URLs for Generic Views

In **snippets/urls.py**, link these views to URLs by creating path entries:

```
from django.urls import path

from .views import SnippetListView, SnippetCreateView
```

```
urlpatterns = [
 path('', SnippetListView.as_view(), name='snippet_list'),
 path('create/', SnippetCreateView.as_view(), name='snippet_create'),
]
```

These URL patterns connect the list and create views to their respective paths, making them accessible via the web. The **ListView** and **CreateView** examples demonstrate how straightforward it is to list objects and handle form submissions with Django, allowing for rapid development without sacrificing functionality or flexibility.

Recipe 6: Creating Custom Middleware for Request Processing

Scenario

When it comes to processing requests and responses on a global scale, Django's middleware is your best bet. Logging, user authentication, and data preprocessing are just a few of the many features that this flexible tool can implement. There may be times when our app requires you to do something specific with each request or response, such as keeping tabs on request statistics, changing request objects, or setting different response headers. To keep your application clean and easy to maintain, you can encapsulate this logic in custom middleware and use it again and again.

Desired Solution

Understanding Middleware Structure

A middleware in Django is a class that defines one or more of the following methods: **__init__** (for setup, no arguments), **__call__** (to get a response for each request), and various hook methods (**process_view**, **process_exception**, **process_template_response**, etc.) to hook into different phases of the request/response lifecycle.

Implementing a Simple Custom Middleware

Suppose you want to add a custom header to every response in GitforGits, indicating the number of code snippets currently available. Following is a sample program on how you could implement this middleware:

```
from django.utils.deprecation import MiddlewareMixin

from .models import Snippet

class SnippetCountMiddleware(MiddlewareMixin):

 def process_response(self, request, response):

 snippet_count = Snippet.objects.count()

 response['X-Snippet-Count'] = str(snippet_count)

 return response
```

This middleware uses the **process_response** method to add a custom header (**X-Snippet-Count**) to every response, showing the current count of **Snippet** objects.

Registering Your Middleware

To activate your custom middleware, add it to the **MIDDLEWARE** setting in your project's **settings.py**. Ensure to reference the middleware using its full import path:

```
MIDDLEWARE = [

 # Default Django middleware...

 'yourapp.middleware.SnippetCountMiddleware',

]
```

Replace **'yourapp.middleware.SnippetCountMiddleware'** with the actual path to your middleware class.

Testing Your Middleware

After adding the middleware to your settings, every response from your Django application should now include the **X-Snippet-Count** header. You can test this by making a request to any endpoint of your application and inspecting the response headers (using browser developer tools or a tool like **curl**). This procedure not only enhances the functionality of GitforGits by providing useful metadata with each response but also demonstrates the flexibility and extensibility of Django's middleware system.

Recipe 7: Securing Views with Permissions and User Checks

Scenario

It is critical that we implement robust security measures to restrict access to features like code snippet editing and administrative functions as our GitforGits app matures. Access to and control over the application's features shouldn't be uniform across all users. Developers can effectively secure views against unauthorized access with Django's robust system for managing user permissions and performing user checks. Users can only engage with content that they have authorization to access, and sensitive actions are safeguarded by implementing these checks.

Desired Solution

Using Decorators for Function-Based Views

Django offers the **@login_required** and **@permission_required** decorators for easy addition of access controls to function-based views. For instance, to restrict access to a view that allows users to edit a snippet, you can use:

```
from django.contrib.auth.decorators import login_required, permission_required

@login_required

@permission_required('snippets.change_snippet', raise_exception=True)

def edit_snippet(request, id):

 # View logic here
```

The **@login_required** decorator ensures that only authenticated users can access the view. The **@permission_required** decorator checks if the user has the specific permission (**'snippets.change_snippet'**) to edit snippets, raising an exception and redirecting to a 403 Forbidden page if not.

Utilizing Mixins for Class-Based Views

For class-based views, Django provides mixins like **LoginRequiredMixin** and **PermissionRequiredMixin** to enforce access controls. Following is a sample program on how to apply them to a class-based view for editing snippets:

```
from django.contrib.auth.mixins import LoginRequiredMixin, PermissionRequiredMixin
from django.views.generic import UpdateView
from .models import Snippet
from .forms import SnippetForm
class EditSnippetView(LoginRequiredMixin, PermissionRequiredMixin, UpdateView):
 model = Snippet
 form_class = SnippetForm
 template_name = 'snippets/snippet_edit.html'
 permission_required = ('snippets.change_snippet',)
 # Additional view configuration...
```

This combination ensures that only authenticated users with the correct permission can access the view. The view itself is an **UpdateView** for editing **Snippet** instances, leveraging Django's generic views for streamlined development.

Custom User Checks

Beyond built-in permissions, you might need custom logic for user checks. This can be done by directly examining properties of the **request.user** object in your view:

```
def custom_snippet_view(request, id):
 if not request.user.is_staff:
 return HttpResponseForbidden("You must be staff to view this.")
 # View logic for staff users...
```

The above sample program demonstrates a simple staff check, restricting access to the view for non-staff users. This recipe is crucial for maintaining the integrity and security of your application as it scales and evolves. Through the use of decorators, mixins, and custom checks, Django offers a flexible and powerful system for managing access control with a variety of user roles and permissions.

Summary

Managing web requests efficiently and mapping URLs to views are two of Django's powerful features that were explored in depth in this chapter. We set out on this adventure by exploring dynamic URL routing techniques, which teach you how to build sophisticated and adaptable URL patterns based on the content being delivered. In order to build clean, maintainable URL schemes that improve user navigation and application scalability, this fundamental skill is required of all Django developers. We learned namespacing, a method for organizing URL patterns across various apps in a project, and advanced URL configurations to further improve our URL management toolbox. Maintaining consistency and clarity as projects become more involved requires this approach to simplify URL reversal within views and templates and prevent naming collisions.

We continued our exploration of user interaction management in this chapter, which demonstrated Django's flexibility by providing practical demonstration of form data handling with both class-based and function-based views. We worked through real-world examples to understand how to use ListView and CreateView, two of Django's generic views, to accomplish typical web development tasks with little code. In addition to speeding up development, this method emphasizes Django's DRY principle by encouraging code reusability and maintainability. In addition, by developing our own request processing middleware, we were able to access previously inaccessible application-wide features like request logging and response object modification, demonstrating how versatile Django is for handling the request-response cycle.

Ensuring the security of sensitive information and functionalities within web applications was emphasized at the end of this chapter with the topic of securing views with permissions and user checks. Developers can build secure, robust applications that protect user data and functionality from unauthorized access by using Django's built-in decorators and mixins and custom user checks. We gained a deeper understanding of Django's URL dispatcher and views, and we gained practical skills and best practices for developing secure, user-friendly, and dynamic web applications with each recipe in this chapter.

Chapter 4: Templates, Static Files, and Media Management

Introduction

This chapter moves on to address how Django can manage both static and dynamic content, as well as the presentation layer. This chapter aims to enhance the skills and expertise related to developing interactive user interfaces that are both responsive and dynamic, all while making sure that the application's resources are managed efficiently. In order to ensure performance, maintainability, and a good user experience while developing apps, it is essential to have the capability to handle media, static files, and templates. Working with Django's templating engine, managing static and media files, and optimizing content delivery are all topics covered in this chapter through a series of recipes.

We look at how to use Django's template engine to make reusable, modular templates. We start by looking at Creating Advanced Template Inheritance and Filters. This makes the codebase easier to maintain by reducing repetition. It is possible to build an application's foundational template structure using advanced inheritance patterns, and then extend and customize it as needed. For an even more adaptable presentation layer, you can make your own template filters to add your own formatting and data manipulation options right in the template itself.

Web project efficiency and organization are directly related to static and media file management. In this recipe, you will learn how to make the most of Django's built-in features for managing static and media files, such as optimizing the delivery of static files and dealing with user-uploaded media. In the end, this improves the application's performance by making sure users get resources fast and efficiently.

The capacity to encapsulate complicated logic into reusable template tags is introduced in Creating Custom Template Tags for Dynamic Content, which further enhances dynamic content delivery. While keeping the robust dynamic content generation capabilities, this makes the templates simpler and easier to read. In addition, optimizing template loading and implementing caching strategies for templates both aim to make Django applications faster and more efficient. Optimizing template loading ensures that templates are processed as efficiently as possible, reducing page load times and improving the user experience. Caching strategies, on the other hand, store rendered templates or portions of them, reducing server load.

This chapter will ensure that you gauge comprehensive insights in how to effectively manage templates, static files, and media in Django, enabling them to create visually appealing, fast, and efficient web applications.

Recipe 1: Creating Advanced Template Inheritance and Filters

Scenario

Having the ability to personalize content for individual pages and keeping the application's overall style constant are common challenges. For this reason, it is essential to have a framework for templates that allows for the greatest possible degree of personalization while reducing complexity and duplication. Thanks to advanced template inheritance, developers can make a base template with common parts like headers, footers, and navigation, and then use child templates to add to or change specific blocks of content. In addition, by using custom template filters, you can format or transform context variables directly within the templates, which significantly improves the display of data.

Desired Solution

Defining a Base Template

Start by creating a base template that includes common elements and defines blocks for overriding. In **templates/base.html**, structure your HTML with named blocks using the **{% block block_name %}{% endblock %}** tags:

```
<!DOCTYPE html>

<html lang="en">

<head>

 <meta charset="UTF-8">

 <title>{% block title %}GitforGits{% endblock %}</title>

</head>

<body>

 <header>

 <!-- Common header content -->

 </header>

 {% block content %}

 <!-- Default content goes here if not overridden -->

 {% endblock %}
```

```
<footer>
<!-- Common footer content -->
</footer>
</body>
</html>
```

Creating Child Templates

Child templates extend the base template and override specific blocks as needed. For example, to create a specific page, you'd start the child template with **{% extends "base.html" %}** and then redefine the blocks you want to customize:

```
{% extends "base.html" %}
{% block title %}Snippet Details{% endblock %}
{% block content %}
<h1>Snippet Details</h1>
<!-- Specific content for the snippet details page -->
{% endblock %}
```

Implementing Custom Template Filters

Sometimes, you'll need to format data in a way that is not supported by Django's built-in template filters. You can create custom filters by defining a function in a **templatetags/your_custom_filters.py** file within your app:

```
from django import template
register = template.Library()
@register.filter(name='custom_date')
def custom_date(value):
```

```
# Transform the value into a custom date format

return value.strftime("%Y-%m-%d at %H:%M")
```

Use your custom filter in templates with the | character followed by the filter's name:

```
Published on: {{ snippet.created_at|custom_date }}
```

To sum up, developers can significantly cut down on code duplication and improve the presentation logic of their Django apps by using advanced template inheritance and custom filters. This approach simplifies development and makes applications easy to maintain and extend.

Recipe 2: Performing Efficient Handling of Static and Media Files

Scenario

For efficiency and effectiveness, it is critical to manage media files (photos, documents submitted by users) and static assets (CSS, JavaScript) well. Media files can significantly increase user engagement, but static files are necessary for styling and integrating your site. But sluggish load times, disorganized files, and security holes are all results of mismanaged files. Problematically, getting these files into Django in a way that doesn't slow down the site or compromise its security is a major undertaking.

Desired Solution

Configuring Static Files

Django provides robust mechanisms for handling static files. The first step is to define where your static files will be stored and how they will be accessed. In your settings.py file, set **STATIC_URL** to specify the URL prefix to access static files, and use **STATICFILES_DIRS** to list directories where Django will search for additional static files, besides each app's 'static' folder:

```
STATIC_URL = '/static/'

STATICFILES_DIRS = [

 BASE_DIR / 'static',
```

```
]
```

For production, you should also set **STATIC_ROOT**, where Django will collect all static files using the **collectstatic** command:

```
STATIC_ROOT = BASE_DIR / 'staticfiles'
```

Managing Media Files

Handling user-uploaded files requires setting up MEDIA_ROOT and MEDIA_URL in your settings.py file. **MEDIA_ROOT** is the filesystem path where these files will be stored, and **MEDIA_URL** is the URL prefix for serving these files:

```
MEDIA_URL = '/media/'

MEDIA_ROOT = BASE_DIR / 'media'
```

In production, ensure your web server is configured to serve the files in **MEDIA_ROOT** at the **MEDIA_URL** path. For development, you can add a URL pattern to serve media files:

```
from django.conf import settings

from django.conf.urls.static import static

urlpatterns = [

 # ... your URL patterns

] + static(settings.MEDIA_URL, document_root=settings.MEDIA_ROOT)
```

Using a Content Delivery Network (CDN)

For improved performance, especially in production, consider serving your static and media files through a Content Delivery Network (CDN). This involves uploading your files to a CDN service and adjusting **STATIC_URL** and/or **MEDIA_URL** to point to the CDN. Using a CDN can significantly reduce load times by serving files from a location close to the user and reducing the bandwidth load on your server.

Recipe 3: Creating Custom Template Tags for Dynamic Content

Scenario

The built-in template tags and filters in Django aren't going to cut it when your app gets more advanced; you'll need to incorporate more sophisticated data manipulations into your templates. You might require a different way to show the most recent code snippets, real-time statistics aggregation, or even the ability to apply custom formatting to user-generated content. By removing labor-intensive tasks from the presentation layer, custom template filters and tags can encapsulate this logic, resulting in more robust and streamlined templates.

Desired Solution

Setting Up Custom Template Tags and Filters

First, you need to create a module within your app to house these custom elements. In your **snippets** app (or whichever app you are working on), create a directory named **templatetags**. Django requires an **__init__.py** file inside this directory to recognize it as a valid Python module, so don't forget to add one. Then, create a Python file for your tags and filters, for example, **snippet_tags.py**.

Writing a Custom Template Tag

Assume that you want to create a custom template tag that fetches the latest code snippets. Inside **snippet_tags.py**, you'd start with:

```
from django import template

from snippets.models import Snippet

register = template.Library()

@register.simple_tag

def get_latest_snippets(count=5):

 return Snippet.objects.order_by('-created_at')[:count]
```

This defines a simple tag called **get_latest_snippets** that returns the latest snippets. You specify the number of snippets you want with the **count** parameter.

Using Your Custom Template Tag in Templates

To use this new tag within a template, you first need to load the tag library with **{% load snippet_tags %}** at the top of your template file. Then, you can use your tag as follows:

```
{% load snippet_tags %}

<ul>

{% get_latest_snippets as latest_snippets %}

{% for snippet in latest_snippets %}

 <li>{{ snippet.title }}</li>

{% endfor %}

</ul>
```

This loads the **get_latest_snippets** tag, calls it to retrieve the latest snippets, and iterates over these snippets to display their titles. This method allows you to abstract complex logic into reusable components, keeping your templates focused on presentation rather than data manipulation. Your application can dynamically now render content based on complex criteria or transformations without cluttering your templates with Python code.

Recipe 4: Implementing Caching Strategies for Templates

Scenario

Your server's load will increase once a certain amount of traffic reaches it. Particularly for dynamic content that needs database access or complicated computation to render, this can cause response times to be slower. By reducing the need to recompute costly operations on each request and temporarily storing their output, caching strategies for templates can significantly improve performance. Caching can improve page loads, user experience, and server load, but it needs careful planning to keep content up-to-date and relevant.

Desired Solution

Understanding Django's Caching Framework

Django comes with a powerful caching framework that supports various backends (e.g., in-memory, file-based, cache servers like Memcached or Redis) and granular control over what gets cached and for how long. Before implementing template caching, decide on a caching backend suitable for your project's needs and configure it in your **settings.py** file.

Template Fragment Caching

For dynamic sites like GitforGits, caching entire pages might not be feasible due to personalized content. However, you can cache portions of a template that are expensive to render but change infrequently. Django provides the **{% cache %}** template tag for this purpose. To use it, first ensure you have the **django.core.cache.backends.locmem.LocMemCache** included in your **INSTALLED_APPS**.

Then, in a template, wrap the cache tag around the content you wish to cache:

```
{% load cache %}

{% cache 300 snippet_details snippet.id %}

 <!-- Expensive operations like database queries -->

 <div>{{ snippet.title }}</div>

 <div>{{ snippet.code }}</div>

{% endcache %}
```

The above sample code caches the details of a snippet for 300 seconds (5 minutes), using the snippet's ID as part of the cache key to ensure the cache is unique to each snippet.

Invalidating Cache

Sometimes, you need to manually invalidate cached content when it changes. Django's caching framework provides methods for this. For example, if a snippet is updated, you can invalidate its cached content by:

```
from django.core.cache import cache

def update_snippet(snippet_id, new_data):

 # Update the snippet logic here

 ...
```

```
# Invalidate the cache

cache_key = f'snippet_details_{snippet_id}'

cache.delete(cache_key)
```

This makes certain that users will be able to view the revised content right away whenever a snippet is modified. One way to keep content up-to-date while still allowing for fast page loads is to cache only the parts of your pages that don't change very often. Follow these steps carefully, and GitforGits will be able to manage increasing traffic and user engagement with ease.

Recipe 5: Optimizing Template Loading

Scenario

Rendering templates is an essential component of providing users with content for a dynamic Django application. The application's overall performance can be significantly affected by how efficiently templates are loaded and rendered, especially as the application grows in complexity and the number of templates increases. A less-than-ideal user experience might result from slow template loading, which impacts both page load times and server load. Improving the loading time of templates is all about finding, compiling, and rendering them with as little overhead as possible. This way, users will get their content as fast as possible.

Desired Solution

Use Template Loaders Efficiently

Django uses template loaders to find and load templates. The order and configuration of these loaders in the **TEMPLATES** setting can impact performance. For most projects, using the **django.template.loaders.cached.Loader** wraps your existing loaders and caches compiled templates, significantly reducing load times:

```
'loaders': [

('django.template.loaders.cached.Loader', [

'django.template.loaders.filesystem.Loader',

'django.template.loaders.app_directories.Loader',
```

```
]),
]
```

This configuration caches templates once they're compiled, so subsequent requests for the same template don't incur the compilation overhead.

Template Inheritance Optimization

Django's template inheritance allows for the reuse of template code, but excessive or deep inheritance chains can lead to performance bottlenecks. Minimize the depth of inheritance where possible, and consider using template includes (**{% include 'some_template.html' %}**) for reusable components rather than basing everything on inheritance. This can reduce the complexity and number of templates that need to be loaded and rendered.

Precompile Templates

For templates that are used very frequently and do not require dynamic context, consider precompiling them into Python code. This approach is advanced and may not be necessary for all projects, but it can reduce the template rendering time to near zero. Tools like **django-template-preprocessor** can assist in this process, but be aware that this technique makes templates static and not suitable for content that changes based on context or requires localization.

Profile Template Rendering

Use Django's template debugging tools, such as the Django Debug Toolbar, to identify slow templates and tags. This can help pinpoint areas where optimization can have the most impact, whether it is simplifying complex templates, reducing the number of template tags, or caching parts of templates that are expensive to render. By carefully managing template loaders, minimizing inheritance depth, considering precompilation for highly static templates, and routinely profiling template rendering, developers can ensure that GitforGits remains fast and responsive as it grows.

Summary

In this chapter, we looked at ways to improve application performance by managing their presentation layer and related assets more efficiently. The chapter started by delving into advanced template inheritance and filters, which offer a strong foundation for making templates that can be reused and maintained. Having this basic understanding is essential for building dynamic websites with consistent functionality and style. Developers can ensure that the application is consistently structured by using Django's templating engine to create hierarchies of templates. This allows child templates to override specific blocks of content, while base templates define the overall structure. With custom template filters, users have even more control over how data is displayed and manipulated within templates, giving them more options for how they see their data.

An important part of web development that affects loading times and resource management is the efficient handling of media and static files, which was the focus of the bulk of the chapter. By providing a systematic way to handle these files, Django streamlines development by making it easy to distinguish between the codebase and static content. Not only does this partition help with organization, but it is also vital for maximizing the client's asset delivery. One way that Django has proven its ability to combine static and dynamic components is by introducing custom template tags. These tags allow users to insert dynamic content into static templates. In order to improve application performance, caching strategies for templates were explored and implemented. It was found that selective caching of template fragments can significantly decrease server load, increase response times, and preserve content freshness.

The chapter concluded with some suggestions for improving template loading, which further demonstrated how critical it is to have fast rendering times. Web applications with time-sensitive user interfaces can benefit significantly from loading and rendering template optimizations. The recipes offered a thorough walkthrough for developers seeking to build web applications that are responsive, efficient, and scalable, with an emphasis on best practices for managing templates, handling static and media files, and optimizing performance. In this chapter, we covered the basics of managing the presentation layer in Django projects and how to use the framework's built-in features to make beautiful, fast-loading websites.

CHAPTER 5: FORMS AND USER INTERACTION

Introduction

In this chapter, we will explore the essential elements of using Django to manage user inputs and interactions. The purpose of this chapter is to provide developers with the understanding as well as skills necessary to design, manage, and optimize forms. To improve functionality and user experience, we will tackle the complex aspects and difficulties of form handling using a set of targeted recipes that cover various techniques and best practices.

In the first recipe, "Using Formsets and Inline Formsets," you'll learn how to manage numerous forms on one page, which will come in handy when you need to create or edit a bunch of similar data objects at once. Consolidating related forms into a cohesive interface is a significant way to improve the user experience and make data entry tasks more efficient. Next, we will take a look at Writing Custom Form Fields and Widgets, which will teach you how to modify form elements to fit your application's needs. This could be to make your UI more engaging, make data input more accurate, or improve usability.

When we use AJAX in Forms for Dynamic User Interfaces, we can make forms that are responsive and interactive, responding to user input in real time without having to reload the page. This method offers personalized and fluid user experiences. When it comes to client-side and server-side validation strategies, using advanced form validation techniques is key to making sure that data collected through forms is accurate, consistent, and secure. The recipe for managing file uploads with forms addresses the difficulties of receiving user files, working around storage, security, and systems for user feedback.

As we go along, we cover the recipe of building multi-step forms, which is useful for collecting detailed data because it covers the design and implementation of complex forms that span multiple pages. Finally, Securing Forms Against Common Attacks stresses the significance of safeguarding forms from multiple security risks, including cross-site request forgery (CSRF), SQL injection, and cross-site scripting (XSS) attacks. This promises to ensure the safe handling of user data and the application's continued security.

By way of these recipes, this chapter expands extensively into Django's form and user interaction features, covering both the tactical and strategic aspects of making forms that are safe, efficient, and easy to use.

Recipe 1: Using Formsets and Inline Formsets

Scenario

Dealing with individual form submissions can get complicated fast when building apps that let users enter multiple records of the same type at once, like adding multiple code snippets in one submission or updating multiple user profiles at the same time. Here, formsets and inline formsets provide a more efficient way to manage numerous forms of the same type inside a single form. If you know how to use formsets correctly, you can improve developer efficiency and user experience by making these situations easier to handle.

Desired Solution

What are Formsets?

Formsets in Django are a layer of abstraction to work with multiple forms on the same page. They allow you to create, process, and validate a set of forms as a group, making it easier to manage forms that share the same fields and validation requirements. Formsets are particularly useful for handling multiple instances of a single model.

Define Your Form

Assuming you have a model **Snippet**, first define a model form:

```
from django.forms import ModelForm

from .models import Snippet

class SnippetForm(ModelForm):

 class Meta:

 model = Snippet

 fields = ['title', 'code', 'language']
```

Create a Formset

Use Django's **formset_factory** to create a formset based on the **SnippetForm**:

```
from django.forms import formset_factory

SnippetFormset = formset_factory(SnippetForm, extra=3)
```

The **extra=3** parameter specifies that the formset should include three empty forms by default.

Handling Formsets in Views

In your view, instantiate the formset and handle it similarly to how you would a single form:

```
from django.shortcuts import render

from .forms import SnippetFormset

def add_snippets(request):

 if request.method == 'POST':

 formset = SnippetFormset(request.POST)

 if formset.is_valid():

 formset.save()

 # Redirect or indicate success

 else:

 formset = SnippetFormset()

 return render(request, 'add_snippets.html', {'formset': formset})
```

Rendering the Formset in Templates

In your template, iterate over the formset to render each form, including management form data:

```
<form method="post">

 {% csrf_token %}

 {{ formset.management_form }}

 {% for form in formset %}

 {{ form.as_p }}

 {% endfor %}

 <button type="submit">Submit</button>

</form>
```

Inline Formsets

Inline formsets are a variation of formsets that are related to a parent model. They are particularly useful for editing related models on the same page as the parent model. Django provides **inlineformset_factory**, which works similarly to **formset_factory** but is designed for handling sets of related objects. You define an inline formset with respect to the parent model and the model form of the child model, specifying the **fk_name** if needed. Formsets are a powerful way to work with multiple forms in Django. They make it easier to create and process instances of forms that are used over and over again.

Recipe 2: Writing Custom Form Fields and Widgets

Scenario

Occasionally, you might find that your application's requirements aren't satisfied by the pre-built form fields and widgets that Django provides. Maybe you are in need of a widget that lets users input data in a special way or a form field that can handle unusual data formats. You can achieve the data handling and user interaction needs of your project with the help of custom form fields and widgets.

Desired Solution

What are Custom Form Fields and Widgets?

Custom form fields in Django allow you to define how data is displayed in a form, how it is validated, and how it converts between its HTML representation and Python objects. Widgets, on the other hand, deal specifically with rendering the HTML and processing user input. Together, they offer the flexibility to create a user interface that matches your application's data and interaction patterns precisely.

Creating a Custom Form Field

Suppose you want to create a custom form field for entering comma-separated emails. This field should validate each email and save them as a list in Python.

```
from django import forms

from django.core.exceptions import ValidationError

from django.core.validators import validate_email
```

```
class CommaSeparatedEmailsField(forms.CharField):

def to_python(self, value):

"""Convert the string of emails into a list."""

if not value:

return []

return [email.strip() for email in value.split(',')]

def validate(self, value):

"""Check if each email in the list is valid."""

super().validate(value)

for email in value:

try:

validate_email(email)

except ValidationError:

raise ValidationError(f"{email} is not a valid email address.")
```

Creating a Custom Widget

To pair with your custom field, you might want a widget that renders a text input but with specific styling or attributes. Following is a sample program on how to create a simple custom widget:

```
from django.forms.widgets import TextInput


class EmailInputWidget(TextInput):

input_type = 'email' # Specifies the HTML input type
```

```
def __init__(self, attrs=None):
super().__init__(attrs)
self.attrs.update({'class': 'email-input', 'placeholder': 'Enter emails separated by commas'})
```

This widget extends the **TextInput** widget, setting the HTML input type to **email** and adding custom classes and placeholders to enhance the user interface.

Using Custom Field and Widget

Incorporate your custom field and widget into a form:

```
class EmailForm(forms.Form):
emails = CommaSeparatedEmailsField(widget=EmailInputWidget())
```

When rendering this form in a template, the **emails** field will use the custom validation logic and display using the custom widget, providing a tailored experience for inputting and validating comma-separated emails.

Recipe 3: Implementing AJAX in Forms for Dynamic User Interfaces

Scenario

Assume you are looking to improve user engagement by letting them know the status of a form right away, without having to refresh the page. For instance, as the user types in a username, it is checked for availability in real-time. However, an asynchronous method of communicating with the server is necessary for this degree of interaction, which has the potential to significantly enhance the user experience. One solution is AJAX, which facilitates asynchronous page updates through data exchange with a web server.

Desired Solution

Setting Up Your Django View

First, create a view in your Django app that responds to AJAX requests. This view might check the database for username availability and return JSON indicating the result.

```
from django.http import JsonResponse

from django.views.decorators.http import require_POST

from .models import User

@require_POST

def check_username(request):

 username = request.POST.get('username', '')

 is_taken = User.objects.filter(username=username).exists()

 return JsonResponse({'is_taken': is_taken})
```

Decorate your view with **@require_POST** to ensure it only responds to POST requests, enhancing security.

Configuring the URL

Add a URL pattern for your AJAX view in your app's **urls.py** file.

```
from django.urls import path

from .views import check_username

urlpatterns = [

 path('ajax/check_username/', check_username, name='ajax_check_username'),

]
```

Creating the AJAX Call with JavaScript

On the client side, use JavaScript to send an AJAX request to the Django view when the user types a username. Include this script in the template that renders your form.

```
<script>
```

```
document.getElementById("username").addEventListener("input", function() {
const username = this.value;
fetch("{% url 'ajax_check_username' %}", {
method: 'POST',
headers: {
'X-Requested-With': 'XMLHttpRequest',
'Content-Type': 'application/json',
'X-CSRFToken': '{{ csrf_token }}',
},
body: JSON.stringify({ username: username })
})
.then(response => response.json())
.then(data => {
if (data.is_taken) {
document.getElementById("username_error").textContent = "Username is taken.";
} else {
document.getElementById("username_error").textContent = "";
}
});
});
</script>
```

Ensure your form includes an element with **id="username_error"** for displaying the availability message. Also, make sure to include **{% csrf_token %}** in your form or fetch call to handle CSRF protection.

Updating Your Form Template

Modify your form template to include the JavaScript and an element to display the username availability message.

```
<input type="text" id="username" name="username">

<div id="username_error"></div>
```

By adding AJAX to your Django forms, you made a user interface that changes based on what the user does and talks to the server in real time, without having to reload the page. This recipe will make your forms more interactive, so users can get feedback right away and your app will be better for them overall.

Recipe 4: Applying Advanced Form Validation Technique

Scenario

Imagine for a second that we are required to build sophisticated validation logic that doesn't make use of Django's default validators. Verifying that a provided code snippet follows specific style rules or does not include prohibited keywords is one example. In order to meet these requirements, it is necessary to fully understand Django's form validation mechanisms. This will enable you to thoroughly review user inputs and ensure that the data submitted to your application is of high quality and integrity.

Desired Solution

Understanding Django's Form Validation

Django forms offer a layered validation system, where you can apply validation at the field level, form level, or even using model-level clean methods. For complex validation scenarios, you might need to use a combination of these to achieve the desired results.

Implementing Field-Level Validation

Start by defining custom validation methods within your form class for specific fields. These methods should be named **clean_<fieldname>()** and must return the cleaned (normalized) value or raise a **ValidationError** if the validation fails.

```
from django import forms

from django.core.exceptions import ValidationError

class SnippetForm(forms.ModelForm):

 class Meta:

 model = Snippet

 fields = ['title', 'code']

 def clean_code(self):

 code = self.cleaned_data['code']

 banned_keywords = ['exec', 'eval']

 for keyword in banned_keywords:

 if keyword in code:

 raise ValidationError(f"Usage of '{keyword}' is not allowed.")

 return code
```

Form-Level Validation

For validations that involve multiple fields (e.g., ensuring two fields are not identical), implement the form's **clean()** method. This method can access the form's **cleaned_data** dictionary to perform cross-field checks.

```
def clean(self):

 cleaned_data = super().clean()

 title = cleaned_data.get("title")
```

```
code = cleaned_data.get("code")
if title and code and title.lower() in code.lower():
raise ValidationError(
"The code snippet should not contain the title."
)
return cleaned_data
```

Custom Validators

For reusable validation logic, consider defining custom validator functions that can be applied to multiple form fields or even across different forms.

```
def validate_not_empty(value):
if not value.strip():
raise ValidationError("This field cannot be empty.")
```

Then, use this validator in your form fields as needed:

```
title = forms.CharField(validators=[validate_not_empty])
```

Utilizing Model's clean Method:

You can also define a **clean** method in your model for an extra layer of validation that is closely tied to your data logic. This is especially useful for enforcing constraints that should apply regardless of the form or method used to create or update an instance. Make sure all form submissions are properly validated according to both basic and advanced rules by using Django's robust validation framework. In addition to making sure that your GitforGits project's data is consistent and of high quality, this also improves the user experience by making it easier to see when they've made a mistake.

Recipe 5: Handling File Uploads with Forms

Scenario

One of the challenges you'll encounter when adding support for users to upload code snippets as files is ensuring the safe and efficient handling of file uploads. There are a lot of things to think about when uploading files, including checking the file type and size, storing the files securely, and providing users with feedback on whether the upload was successful or not. To avoid security holes, make good use of server resources, and guarantee a seamless user experience, proper handling is essential.

Desired Solution

Modifying the Model to Support File Uploads

Start by adding a file field to your **Snippet** model. Django's **FileField** or **ImageField** (for images) makes storing uploaded files straightforward. You might also want to store metadata like the upload's original filename.

```
from django.db import models

class Snippet(models.Model):

 # Other fields...

 file = models.FileField(upload_to='snippets/')
```

The **upload_to** argument specifies a subdirectory of your **MEDIA_ROOT** setting where uploaded files will be stored.

Creating a Form for File Upload

Update your **SnippetForm** to include the file field. If using a **ModelForm**, the field is automatically included; just ensure your form's HTML includes **enctype="multipart/form-data"** to support file uploads.

```
<form method="post" enctype="multipart/form-data">

 {{ form.as_p }}

 <button type="submit">Upload</button>

</form>
```

Handling File Uploads in Your View

Modify the view that processes the form to handle the uploaded file securely. When the form is valid, you can access the file through **request.FILES**.

```
from django.shortcuts import render, redirect

from .forms import SnippetForm

def upload_snippet(request):

 if request.method == 'POST':

 form = SnippetForm(request.POST, request.FILES)

 if form.is_valid():

 form.save()

 return redirect('snippets:snippet_list')

 else:

 form = SnippetForm()

 return render(request, 'snippets/upload_form.html', {'form': form})
```

Note the inclusion of **request.FILES** in the form instantiation, necessary for file processing.

Validating Uploaded Files

For security and usability, implement validation on the uploaded file, either by overriding the **clean_<fieldname>()** method in your form or by using a custom validator. You might want to check the file size, file type, or scan for malicious content.

```
def clean_file(self):

 file = self.cleaned_data['file']

 if file.size > 1024 * 1024 * 5:

 raise ValidationError("File size must be under 5MB")
```

```
if not file.name.endswith('.py'):
    raise ValidationError("Only Python files are allowed.")
    return file
```

Ensure your template and view logic provide clear feedback on the status of file uploads, including success messages and error details for failed validations. By following these steps, you can safely integrate file upload capabilities into GitforGits, expanding its functionality and user engagement.

Recipe 6: Building Multi-Step Forms

Scenario

Think of a multi-part form for submitting thorough code reviews as an example of a user submission process that could benefit from your attention-grabbing design. By dividing a long process into smaller, more manageable steps, multi-step forms can enhance the user experience, making it easier for users to complete and decreasing the likelihood that they will become frustrated. The maintenance of state, validation of input at each step, and consolidation of the final submission are all made more difficult when data flows across numerous form pages.

Desired Solution

Designing the Form Flow

Plan out the sequence of steps, determining what information is collected at each stage. For a code review submission, you might have steps like "Code Details," "Review Questions," and "Submit." Each step can be represented by a distinct Django form class.

Storing Intermediate Data

Utilize Django's session framework to temporarily store data between steps. This approach allows you to save the user's input at each stage without persisting it to the database until the final submission.

```
# In your view handling the first step
if form.is_valid():
    request.session['step1_data'] = form.cleaned_data
```

```
return redirect('next_form_url')
```

Handling Each Step

Create views for each step of the process. In each view, initialize the form with session data if available (for editing previous responses) and save the form data to the session upon successful submission.

```
# Handling the second step

initial_data = request.session.get('step2_data', {})

form = Step2Form(initial=initial_data)

if request.method == 'POST':

 form = Step2Form(request.POST)

 if form.is_valid():

 request.session['step2_data'] = form.cleaned_data

 return redirect('final_step_url')
```

Consolidating Data for Final Submission

In the final step, consolidate data from all steps, stored in the session, to create or update the relevant model instance(s). This might involve populating a complex model or related models with the collected data.

```
if request.method == 'POST':

 # Assume all form validations have passed

 all_data = {**request.session['step1_data'], **request.session['step2_data']}

 new_review = CodeReview.objects.create(**all_data)

 # Clear the session data related to the form process

 del request.session['step1_data']
```

```
del request.session['step2_data']

return redirect('review_success_url')
```

It is crucial to manage the session data carefully to avoid stale or incomplete submissions. Consider adding mechanisms to clear session data at the start of the process or upon completion/cancellation.

Recipe 7: Securing Forms Against Common Attacks

Scenario

As a main point of entry for users, forms are frequently the target of attacks like SQL Injection, Cross-Site Request Forgery (CSRF), and Cross-Site Scripting (XSS). Failing to adequately resolve these vulnerabilities could jeopardize user data and application integrity. The confidence and safety of the application users depend on the implementation of strong security measures to ward off these typical attacks.

Desired Solution

Preventing Cross-Site Scripting (XSS)

XSS attacks involve injecting malicious scripts into web pages viewed by other users. Django templates escape variables by default, which protects against XSS by ensuring that any input is rendered as text rather than executable HTML/JavaScript. Always use Django's template system to display form data or any user-generated content. For content that includes HTML and still needs to be safe, consider using the **bleach** library to sanitize the input, allowing only specified tags and attributes.

```
import bleach


def clean_user_input(content):

 return bleach.clean(content, tags=['p', 'b', 'i', 'u', 'a'], attributes=['href', 'title'], strip=True)
```

Protecting Against Cross-Site Request Forgery (CSRF)

CSRF attacks trick a user into executing unwanted actions on a web application in which they're authenticated. Django counters CSRF attacks by including a secret token with each form submission, which must be present and correct for the form to be processed. Ensure **{% csrf_token %}** is included within every form in your templates. Django's middleware checks this token automatically, but always verify that **django.middleware.csrf.CsrfViewMiddleware** is enabled in your **MIDDLEWARE** settings.

Guarding Against SQL Injection

SQL Injection attacks involve inserting or "injecting" an SQL query via the input data from the client to the application. Django's ORM, by default, uses parameterized queries, which effectively protect against SQL injection. Ensure that any raw SQL queries also use parameterization and avoid directly including user input in query strings.

Validating and Sanitizing Input

Beyond leveraging Django's built-in protections, always validate and sanitize user input to enforce constraints and remove potentially harmful data. Use Django forms and model field options to enforce data types, lengths, and formats. Custom validators can provide additional layers of validation specific to your application's needs.

Your Django application's forms will be protected from typical web vulnerabilities if you follow these security practices. Additionally, it is critical to regularly update Django and any third-party packages to the most recent versions. This will guarantee that you have the most recent security fixes.

Summary

In this chapter, we covered the complex methods of form handling in Django, which are essential for enabling dynamic user interactions inside the application. In this chapter, we learned how to use Formsets and Inline Formsets to manage multiple forms at once in Django. This makes tasks like handling bulk submissions or edits much easier. In this first section, we learned about Django's capabilities to simplify complicated data collection processes by demonstrating its adaptability to user inputs. We further demonstrated Django's adaptability in our exploration of writing custom form fields and widgets. By creating bespoke form elements that meet the needs of specific applications, we can improve functionality and user engagement while creating a tailored user experience.

The chapter continued by shedding light on how AJAX was incorporated into Forms, which was a game-changer for the user interface dynamics as it allowed for asynchronous data submissions. By providing real-time feedback and interaction without the need for a full-page refresh, this technique significantly improves the user experience and keeps users engaged and informed.

Strong data validation, which includes thorough checks at the field and form levels to guarantee the authenticity and safety of user-submitted information, was a common theme in the Advanced Form Validation Techniques recipe. In order to simplify the process of receiving user-generated content, the recipe on Handling File Uploads with Forms addressed the challenges of secure storage, validation, and user feedback mechanisms.

The chapter ended with the recipe "Building Multi-Step Forms and Securing Forms Against Common Attacks." The areas covered included improving the user experience by using segmented data collection processes and protecting form submissions from common web vulnerabilities such as XSS, CSRF, and SQL Injection. In order to build reliable web applications, these sections emphasized the need for careful form design and rigorous security measures.

CHAPTER 6: AUTHENTICATION AND AUTHORIZATION

Introduction

For Django applications, this chapter goes into detail about the most necessary components of security and user management. In order to ensure safe and customized user interactions with the platform, this chapter is designed to provide developers with all the knowledge they need to create strong authentication and authorization systems. This chapter provides best practices and practical solutions for a variety of authentication and authorization scenarios through a series of detailed recipes.

The chapter begins with an overview of the fundamental procedures involved in modifying the default user model of Django to align more closely with the specific requirements of a given application. This may involve the addition of additional fields or methods. If your app needs more advanced user attributes than what Django offers, this customization is a must. After this, the recipe, "Implementing Advanced User Authentication Flows," looks into methods for improving the typical authentication procedure, such as email-based authentication and adding extra checks or stages to make the process more secure and better for the user.

The next recipe allows application-wide access control for granular permissions that reflect the variety of user roles. With the integration of OAuth and Social Authentication, the application can reach a wider audience and simplify the login process for users by letting them sign in using third-party providers like Google or Facebook.

Following this, you'll find solutions on how to manage user sessions and cookies for keeping stateful interactions alive in a stateless web setting; another recipe on how to customize Django authentication forms so that you can have a unique authentication user interface. With Two-Factor Authentication recipe, an extra safeguard is added, and the likelihood of unwanted access is drastically diminished. Lastly, making sure users can safely access and recover their accounts is covered in Managing User Account Activation and Password Reset, which covers essential features for user account management.

Developing an authentication and authorization system that is secure, efficient, and easy to use is the main focus of this chapter, rather than merely utilizing Django's built-in features.

Recipe 1: Setting up Custom User Models

Scenario

At some point, every application will demand a more personalized user management system. Although Django's default user model is strong, it might not meet all of your application's needs. For example, your app might need to add extra user information like a bio, profile picture, or social media links. Building a unique user model from the ground up is essential if you want to meet these demands and improve the user experience. You can define user attributes with more flexibility and your application will be future-proofed against evolving requirements with this approach.

Desired Solution

Create a Custom User Model

Begin by defining your custom user model in your models.py. It is recommended to extend AbstractBaseUser and optionally PermissionsMixin to get full control over the user model while retaining Django's permissions framework.

```
from django.contrib.auth.models import AbstractBaseUser, PermissionsMixin,
BaseUserManager

class CustomUserManager(BaseUserManager):

 def create_user(self, email, password=None, **extra_fields):

 if not email:

 raise ValueError('The Email field must be set')

 email = self.normalize_email(email)

 user = self.model(email=email, **extra_fields)

 user.set_password(password)

 user.save(using=self._db)

 return user

 def create_superuser(self, email, password, **extra_fields):

 extra_fields.setdefault('is_staff', True)

 extra_fields.setdefault('is_superuser', True)

 return self.create_user(email, password, **extra_fields)

class CustomUser(AbstractBaseUser, PermissionsMixin):

 email = models.EmailField(unique=True)
```

```
is_active = models.BooleanField(default=True)

is_staff = models.BooleanField(default=False)

# Additional fields here

objects = CustomUserManager()

USERNAME_FIELD = 'email'

REQUIRED_FIELDS = []
```

Update settings.py

Inform Django about your custom user model by setting the AUTH_USER_MODEL in your project's settings.py file.

```
AUTH_USER_MODEL = 'myapp.CustomUser'
```

Replace 'myapp' with the actual app name where your custom user model is defined.

Migrations

After defining your custom user model and updating your settings, generate and apply migrations to create the corresponding database table.

```
python manage.py makemigrations

python manage.py migrate
```

Adapting the Admin Interface

To manage users via Django's admin, define a custom ModelAdmin class for your user model in admin.py.

```
from django.contrib import admin

from django.contrib.auth.admin import UserAdmin

from .models import CustomUser
```

```
class CustomUserAdmin(UserAdmin):
 model = CustomUser
 list_display = ['email', 'is_staff', 'is_active']
 # Configure additional fields as needed
admin.site.register(CustomUser, CustomUserAdmin)
```

By creating a one-of-a-kind user model, your app is able to accommodate specific user characteristics and actions, providing the groundwork for an individualized and safe experience.

Recipe 2: Implementing Advanced User Authentication Flows

Scenario

At any stage throughout an application's lifetime, an increasingly complex user authentication flow may be required to boost security and user experience. Maybe you are interested in adding security features like mail verification, login without a password, or multiple factor authentication. Such complex flows demand a change from Django's standard authentication methods, requiring the development of custom logic to manage the extra checks and steps.

Desired Solution

Email Verification Process

After a user signs up, enhance security by verifying their email address. Extend the user model to include an email verification flag and a unique verification token.

```
from django.db import models
from django.contrib.auth.models import AbstractBaseUser
from django.utils.crypto import get_random_string
class CustomUser(AbstractBaseUser):
 email_verified = models.BooleanField(default=False)
```

```
verification_token = models.CharField(max_length=100, blank=True)
def save(self, *args, **kwargs):
if not self.verification_token:
self.verification_token = get_random_string(50)
super().save(*args, **kwargs)
```

Sending Verification Email

After registration, send an email containing a verification link with the token. Use Django's email utilities to send this email and a view to handle the verification link click.

```
from django.core.mail import send_mail
from django.urls import reverse
from django.shortcuts import redirect
def send_verification_email(user):
verification_url = reverse('verify_email', args=[user.verification_token])
send_mail(
'Verify your GitforGits account',
f'Please verify your account by clicking this link: {verification_url}',
'no-reply@gitforgits.com',
[user.email],
fail_silently=False,
)
def verify_email(request, token):
```

```
 user = CustomUser.objects.get(verification_token=token)
 user.email_verified = True
 user.save()
 return redirect('login')
```

Passwordless Login

Implement a passwordless login system by sending a one-time use link or token to the user's email.

```
def send_login_email(request):
 email = request.POST['email']
 user = CustomUser.objects.get(email=email)
 token = get_random_string(50)
 user.login_token = token
 user.save()
 login_url = reverse('passwordless_login', args=[token])
 send_mail(
 'Your login link for GitforGits',
 f'Click here to log in: {login_url}',
 'no-reply@gitforgits.com',
 [email],
 fail_silently=False,
 )
 # Inform user that email was sent
```

```
def passwordless_login(request, token):
 user = CustomUser.objects.get(login_token=token)
 user.login_token = ''
 user.save()
 login(request, user)
 return redirect('dashboard')
```

Ensure your user model has fields for login_token and handle token cleanup for security. Implementing advanced authentication flows in Django adds layers of security and usability to your application, accommodating modern web practices and user expectations. Whether through email verification, passwordless login, or other methods, these enhancements are crucial for building trust and maintaining the integrity of user data.

Recipe 3: Executing Role-Based Permissions and Groups

Scenario

Different user roles, such as administrators, content creators, and regular users, will need different levels of access and permissions as the application progresses. In order to keep the platform secure and intact, it is essential to manage these roles and the permissions that come with them. To efficiently manage user capabilities and access rights throughout the application, Django's built-in groups and permissions framework provides a robust solution for implementing role-based access control (RBAC).

Desired Solution

Defining User Groups and Permissions

Start by identifying the roles needed within your application and the specific permissions each role requires. Permissions in Django are typically tied to models and can be automatically generated for add, change, delete, and view operations. For custom permissions or more granular control, you can define them directly in your models.

```
from django.db import models

class Snippet(models.Model):

 # Model fields

 class Meta:

 permissions = [

 ("approve_snippet", "Can approve snippets"),

 ("feature_snippet", "Can mark snippets as featured"),

 ]
```

Creating Groups and Assigning Permissions

Use Django's admin site or shell to create groups corresponding to your roles and assign the relevant permissions to each group. For example, create a "Content Creators" group with permissions to add and change snippets.

```
from django.contrib.auth.models import Group, Permission

# Creating a group for content creators

content_creators_group, created = Group.objects.get_or_create(name='Content Creators')

# Fetching model permissions

add_snippet_perm = Permission.objects.get(codename='add_snippet')

change_snippet_perm = Permission.objects.get(codename='change_snippet')

# Assigning permissions to the group

content_creators_group.permissions.add(add_snippet_perm, change_snippet_perm)
```

Assigning Users to Groups

Assign users to the appropriate groups based on their roles. This can be done programmatically or through the Django admin interface.

```
from django.contrib.auth.models import User

# Assuming you have a user instance

user = User.objects.get(username='johndoe')

user.groups.add(content_creators_group)
```

Checking Permissions in Views

Within your views, leverage Django's permission-checking utilities to control access. You can use decorators for function-based views and mixins for class-based views.

```
from django.contrib.auth.decorators import permission_required

from django.contrib.auth.mixins import PermissionRequiredMixin

from django.views.generic import View

# For function-based views

@permission_required('snippets.add_snippet', raise_exception=True)

def add_snippet(request):

 # View logic

# For class-based views

class FeatureSnippetView(PermissionRequiredMixin, View):

 permission_required = 'snippets.feature_snippet'

 # View logic
```

With Django's role-based permissions and groups, you can build an authorization system that is secure, scalable, and compatible with GitforGits's varied requirements. Users' interactions with the platform should be in line with their responsibilities, which improves security and user experience. This can be achieved by clearly defining roles and carefully managing permissions.

Recipe 4: Implementing OAuth and Social Authentication

Scenario

Our application's login process could use some improvement, so we're considering integrating OAuth and social authentication as a strategic move. This method eliminates the need for users to generate and remember a separate set of login credentials by letting them sign in with their preexisting social media accounts. Not only does using OAuth and social authentication make signing in easier, but it also has the ability to boost registration rates by capitalizing on the trust and familiarity that users already have with these platforms. However, additional security considerations and careful integration with third-party services are necessary for setting up social authentication.

Desired Solution

Choosing a Library

Django-allauth is a popular package that provides comprehensive support for social authentication, handling the complexities of OAuth protocols and integrating with a wide range of providers. Start by installing Django-allauth in your virtual environment:

```
pip install django-allauth
```

Configuring `settings.py`

Add django.contrib.sites, allauth, allauth.account, and allauth.socialaccount to your INSTALLED_APPS. Also, configure the Django sites framework by setting SITE_ID, typically to 1, and add allauth's authentication backends:

```
INSTALLED_APPS = [

 # Other apps...

'django.contrib.sites',

'allauth',
```

```
 'allauth.account',
 'allauth.socialaccount',
 # Providers (e.g., Google, Facebook)
 'allauth.socialaccount.providers.google',
]

AUTHENTICATION_BACKENDS = [
 'django.contrib.auth.backends.ModelBackend',
 'allauth.account.auth_backends.AuthenticationBackend',
]
SITE_ID = 1
```

Updating URLs

Include allauth URLs in your project's urls.py to make the authentication views available:

```
urlpatterns = [
 # Other URLs...
 path('accounts/', include('allauth.urls')),
]
```

Configuring Providers

Visit the admin panel to configure the social applications (e.g., Google, Facebook) with the credentials obtained from their developer consoles. This typically involves specifying a client ID and secret key and setting the callback URLs as required by each provider.

Customizing Templates and Flows

While Django-allauth provides default templates, customizing them to match your application's look and feel can offer a seamless user experience. Explore allauth's template customization options to integrate social login buttons and user flow seamlessly into GitforGits.

Handling Post-Login Actions

Consider implementing signals or overriding allauth's adapters to perform actions after a successful login, such as fetching additional user information from the provider or creating user profiles within your application.

This entire method streamlines the login process and follows current web standards, which improves the user experience and may lead to more engagement on the platform.

Recipe 5: Managing User Sessions and Cookies

Scenario

The stateless HTTP protocol relies on sessions and cookies to keep state, which allows for secure authentication and personalized user experiences. When these components are handled correctly, our application allows users to navigate without any issues, and their authentication state and preferences are saved from one visit to the next. Furthermore, in order to optimize performance and maintain security standards, it is essential to manage sessions and cookies mindfully. This will prevent vulnerabilities like session hijacking.

Desired Solution

Configuring Django Session Framework

Django's session framework provides a robust mechanism for storing information on the server side, with a key referenced in a user's cookie. Ensure your Django project is configured to use the desired session engine in settings.py:

```
# Use database-backed sessions

SESSION_ENGINE = 'django.contrib.sessions.backends.db'

# Or, for better performance with cache setup

SESSION_ENGINE = 'django.contrib.sessions.backends.cached_db'
```

Run python manage.py migrate if using database-backed sessions to set up the necessary database tables.

Session Security Settings

Configure session security settings in settings.py to enhance security. For instance, use HTTPS for cookie transmission, set the session cookie as HttpOnly to prevent client-side scripts from accessing the session ID, and enable SESSION_EXPIRE_AT_BROWSER_CLOSE to clear sessions when the browser is closed:

```
SESSION_COOKIE_SECURE = True

SESSION_COOKIE_HTTPONLY = True

SESSION_EXPIRE_AT_BROWSER_CLOSE = True
```

Managing Sessions in Views

Use Django's session framework to store and retrieve data within your views. For example, storing a user's theme preference might involve:

```
def set_theme(request):

 theme = request.GET.get('theme', 'light')

 request.session['theme'] = theme

 return HttpResponse(f"Theme set to {theme}")
```

Customizing Cookies

While sessions are suitable for most use cases, directly setting cookies on the client may be necessary for certain scenarios, such as tracking anonymous user preferences. Use Django's response objects to set cookies:

```
def set_preference(request):

 response = HttpResponse("Preference saved")

 response.set_cookie('preferred_language', 'python')

 return response
```

Consider cookie attributes such as expires, max_age, secure, and httponly for finer control and enhanced security.

Cookie and Session Cleanup

Regularly clearing expired sessions from the database helps maintain performance. Django includes a management command for this purpose:

```
python manage.py clearsessions
```

Automate this command with a scheduled task (e.g., cron job) to keep the session table optimized.

Improving the security and customization of our application relies heavily on properly managing user sessions and cookies. Supporting the smooth operation of authentication systems, user preferences, and other stateful interactions across the platform, developers can leverage Django's session framework and mindful cookie management to ensure the secure and efficient handling of user data.

Recipe 6: Customizing Django Authentication Forms

Scenario

While Django's built-in authentication forms do the job, they might not be a good fit for your application's specific branding, style, or data collection needs. In addition to collecting more data during registration or login, or giving users more helpful feedback, customizing these forms lets them blend in with the site's design and UX goals.

Desired Solution

Extending Authentication Forms

Begin by extending the existing authentication forms to add custom fields or modify existing ones. For example, to add a 'remember me' option to the login form, you could extend AuthenticationForm:

```
from django import forms

from django.contrib.auth.forms import AuthenticationForm
```

```
class CustomAuthenticationForm(AuthenticationForm):
    remember_me = forms.BooleanField(required=False, label='Remember me')
```

This adds a new field to the form without altering the underlying authentication logic.

Customizing Form Layout and Validation

Override the __init__ method of your custom form to apply custom styling or initialize fields in a specific way. You can also add clean methods to include custom validation for your new fields or override existing validation logic.

```
def __init__(self, *args, **kwargs):
    super(CustomAuthenticationForm, self).__init__(*args, **kwargs)
    self.fields['username'].widget.attrs.update({'class': 'custom-class'})
    self.fields['remember_me'].initial = True
def clean_remember_me(self):
    # Custom validation logic for remember_me
    return self.cleaned_data['remember_me']
```

Integrating Custom Forms into Views

Use your custom form in Django's authentication views by either extending the existing authentication views or by specifying the form explicitly if using class-based views. For example, to use the custom authentication form in a class-based login view:

```
from django.contrib.auth.views import LoginView
class CustomLoginView(LoginView):
    form_class = CustomAuthenticationForm
```

Update your URL configuration to use this custom view instead of the default login view.

Rendering Custom Forms in Templates

Customize the template used by your form to ensure it reflects the added fields and matches the site's styling. Remember to load and display form errors to provide feedback to the user.

```
<form method="post">
 {% csrf_token %}
 {{ form.as_p }}
 <button type="submit">Login</button>
</form>
```

Not only does this recipe improve the aesthetic and practical elements of user authentication, but it also creates chances to collect more data about users and give them more specific feedback, making the platform even more personalized to their needs and expectations.

Recipe 7: Implementing Two-Factor Authentication

Scenario

By incorporating two-factor authentication (2FA), an extra safeguard is created, drastically decreasing the likelihood of unwanted entry. Users are prompted to submit two pieces of identification in order to access their accounts when using two-factor authentication (2FA). This typically involves something the user knows (like a password) and something the user has (like a code sent to their mobile device).

Desired Solution

Choose a 2FA Method

Decide on the methods of 2FA you want to offer. Common options include SMS codes, email codes, or time-based one-time passwords (TOTP) generated by an app like Google Authenticator or Authy. TOTP is a popular choice due to its higher security compared to SMS.

Integrating with a Third-Party Service

For SMS or email-based 2FA, integrate with a third-party service like Twilio or SendGrid. These services offer APIs to send messages or emails containing the 2FA codes. For TOTP, libraries like django-otp or pyotp can be used to generate and verify tokens.

Modifying the User Model

Extend your user model to store 2FA-related information. For TOTP, you might store a secret key for each user.

```
from django.db import models

from django.contrib.auth.models import AbstractUser

import pyotp

class CustomUser(AbstractUser):

 two_factor_enabled = models.BooleanField(default=False)

 otp_secret_key = models.CharField(max_length=100, blank=True, default='')

 def generate_totp_secret(self):

 if not self.otp_secret_key:

 self.otp_secret_key = pyotp.random_base32()

 self.save()
```

2FA Setup and Verification Flow

Create views and templates for users to enable 2FA, including generating a QR code for TOTP that users can scan with their authentication app. Use pyotp to generate the QR code URL.

```
import pyotp

def setup_2fa(request):

 user = request.user

 user.generate_totp_secret()

 otp_uri = pyotp.totp.TOTP(user.otp_secret_key).provisioning_uri(user.email,
issuer_name="GitforGits")
```

```
# Render a template that displays the QR code and a form to verify the token
```

Verifying 2FA at Login

Extend the login process to include a second step for 2FA verification. After the user successfully enters their password, prompt them for their 2FA code. Verify the code against the user's secret key or the code received via SMS/email.

```
def verify_2fa_code(request):
    user = request.user
    token = request.POST.get('token')
    totp = pyotp.TOTP(user.otp_secret_key)
    if totp.verify(token):
        # Log the user in and redirect to the dashboard
    else:
        # Return an error message
```

Installing two-factor authentication makes user accounts on GitforGits much more secure, preventing unauthorized access and boosting user confidence in the platform's safety. Even though it adds another layer of authentication, the increased security is well worth the extra effort, particularly for apps that handle sensitive data or financial transactions.

Recipe 8: Managing User Account Activation and Password Reset

Scenario

The security of user registrations is enhanced through the use of email verification to activate accounts. This process helps to confirm the authenticity of registered email addresses. In the exact same way, a simple method for users to reset their passwords is of the utmost importance for keeping them as customers. To keep users' confidence and safety on the platform, both procedures are essential.

Desired Solution

Account Activation via Email

- User Model Extension: Ensure your user model includes a field for tracking email verification status, such as email_verified = models.BooleanField(default=False).
- Sending Activation Emails: Upon user registration, generate a unique activation token and send an email with a link containing this token. Use Django's built-in send_mail function or a third-party service for email delivery.
- Activation View: Create a view that validates the activation token from the email link, sets the user's email_verified flag to True, and completes the account activation process.
- Email Template: Craft a clear and concise email template for the activation email, including instructions on how to activate the account.

Password Reset Process

- Password Reset Views: Leverage Django's built-in views for password reset: PasswordResetView for submitting the email form, PasswordResetDoneView for confirming that the reset email has been sent, PasswordResetConfirmView for the actual password reset form where the user inputs a new password, and PasswordResetCompleteView for confirming the password has been changed.
- Email Integration: Customize the email template used by PasswordResetView to align with your site's branding and provide clear instructions. Ensure your email backend is correctly configured in Django settings.
- URL Configuration: Include the URLs for Django's password reset views in your project's urls.py. Customize the URL patterns if necessary to fit your site's routing schema.
- Security Considerations: Ensure the password reset process is secure. Django's views already include necessary security checks, such as token validation and expiration.

For both account activation and password reset, customize the templates to provide a consistent user experience that matches your site's design. Include user-friendly messages and instructions. And, implement clear success and error messages throughout the account activation and password reset processes. This feedback is crucial for guiding users through the steps and handling any issues that arise.

Summary

This chapter systematically covered the technicalities of managing user interactions and securing the Django framework. The chapter began by learning how to modify the user model, and then went on to stress the significance of adapting the authentication mechanism to each application's specific requirements. This flexibility allows for the integration of advanced user authentication flows, which improve security and user convenience by incorporating features like passwordless login and email verification. For more in-depth interactions with user data and security protocols, it was necessary to put bespoke user models and authentication flows into practice.

This chapter explored OAuth and role-based permissions in depth, which improved my understanding of how to manage access control and how to use social media for easier user authentication. Successive recipes on session management, cookie customization, and authentication form customization further brought to the point the need for an authentication process that is both secure and easy to use by outlining ways to improve session management for users and make the authentication interface match the aesthetic of the application. The strategic integration of two-factor authentication and the efficient management of account activations and password resets played a critical role in fortifying the security framework of GitforGits. These measures provided additional safeguards against unauthorized access and facilitated the recovery of user accounts.

Each recipe highlighted the importance of a secure, flexible, and user-centric approach to managing user interactions while also providing practical solutions to common authentication and authorization challenges.

CHAPTER 7: DJANGO REST FRAMEWORK FOR APIS

Introduction

Django REST Framework (DRF) is an excellent tool for building APIs that are scalable, resilient, and easy to maintain. This chapter will walk you through the fundamentals of DRF. This chapter intends to provide developers like you with the knowledge necessary to exploit DRF's extensive set of features for effective API creation, addressing frequent scenarios and issues encountered when establishing and managing APIs.

First, we will go over the basics of integrating DRF into your Django project in the Setting up and configuring recipe, which lays the framework for developing APIs. This includes installing DRF, configuring it in your project settings, and defining the architectural choices that will shape your API. In the next recipe, "Building Your First API View," you will learn the fundamentals of exposing your data through a web API. This will be achieved by following the steps to create your first endpoints using DRF's views and routers.

As we go further, Working with Serializers for Complex Data explores the art of converting your Django models to JSON so that APIs may consume them, and the other way around. This is an essential recipe for data sharing in web applications. Your API must be secure and accessible only to authorized users. To do this, you must implement authentication and permissions in your API. This recipe shows how DRF interfaces with Django's authentication system to safeguard your data.

The chapter then moves on to improve API usability and client-side interaction by covering recipe on Customizing Pagination and Filtering, which is an essential strategy for managing huge datasets and giving users control over the data they obtain. Then, you'll be ready to update your API without affecting current users by following the tips provided in Best Practices for API Versioning recipe. This will help you maintain compatibility with older versions of your API while also planning for its future expansion.

For your API to work as intended and fulfill its design requirements, it is crucial to employ thorough testing procedures, as emphasized in recipe 'Testing and Debugging DRF Applications'. This recipe goes into DRF's testing tools and processes for ensuring a stable codebase. Finally, Implementing Throttling and Rate Limiting for APIs addresses the operational side of API administration, preventing overuse and ensuring equal resource distribution among users.

Throughout Chapter 7, the emphasis is on practical, real-world solutions and best practices for building APIs with the DRF. Exploring these recipes will provide developers with a complete overview of DRF's capabilities, ranging from initial setup and basic CRUD operations to advanced features such as security, versioning, and rate limitation. This chapter will teach you how to create high-quality APIs that can be used as the cornerstone for online and mobile applications, laying the groundwork for GitforGits' future growth and success.

Recipe 1: Setting up and Configuring DRF

Scenario

You want to build a set of APIs that will enable programmatic access to the platform's resources—including user profiles, code snippets, and more—in order to make GitforGits more interactive. The DRF is the best toolset for this job because it is versatile, well-documented, and helps with quick development. In order to construct a strong API, you must first install and configure DRF correctly. This includes adding the framework to your Django project and initializing its settings to meet your project's requirements.

Desired Solution

Install DRF

Begin by adding DRF to your project. You can install it using pip:

```
pip install djangorestframework
```

Update Installed Apps

Next, add **'rest_framework'** to the **INSTALLED_APPS** section of your project's **settings.py** file. This step makes Django aware of the DRF application and its components.

```
INSTALLED_APPS = [
 ...
 'rest_framework',
]
```

Configure DRF Settings

DRF comes with a wide range of settings that allow you to customize its behavior to fit your project. In your **settings.py**, you can start by defining some basic configurations under the **REST_FRAMEWORK** setting. For example, setting up default permissions and pagination:

```
REST_FRAMEWORK = {
 'DEFAULT_PERMISSION_CLASSES': [
 'rest_framework.permissions.IsAuthenticatedOrReadOnly',
```

```
],
'DEFAULT_PAGINATION_CLASS':
'rest_framework.pagination.PageNumberPagination',
'PAGE_SIZE': 10,
}
```

These settings specify that by default, API access should be restricted to authenticated users for write operations while allowing read-only access to unauthenticated users, and enable pagination for API responses.

Initial API Routing

Define a URLconf for your API by creating a **urls.py** file in your app directory (if not already present) or the project directory. Use DRF's router classes for easy URL routing of viewsets:

```
from django.urls import include, path
from rest_framework.routers import DefaultRouter
from yourapp import views
router = DefaultRouter()
router.register(r'snippets', views.SnippetViewSet)
urlpatterns = [
 path('api/', include(router.urls)),
]
```

This setup declares a simple API route for accessing snippet resources, assuming you have a **SnippetViewSet** defined in your views.

Enable Browsable API

One of DRF's standout features is its browsable API, which is enabled by default. This allows developers and users to interact with the API directly from their browsers, a great tool for testing and exploring your API's capabilities.

Now that you have DRF set up, you can begin to construct the API views and logic that are unique to GitforGits or any of your applications.

Recipe 2: Building Your First API View

Scenario

Once DRF is set up in the GitforGits project, the first API view may be created. The objective is to create an API endpoint that is both easy to use and effective in retrieving a collection of code snippets. This endpoint is a major step towards making the platform more interactive and service-oriented by exposing GitforGits's resources through an easily-understood API.

Desired Solution

Define a Serializer

Before creating the view, you need a way to convert your model instances into a format that can be easily rendered into JSON or XML for API responses. DRF's serializers handle this task. Define a serializer for your **Snippet** model in a new file **serializers.py** within your app:

```
from rest_framework import serializers

from .models import Snippet

class SnippetSerializer(serializers.ModelSerializer):

 class Meta:

 model = Snippet

 fields = ['id', 'title', 'code', 'created_at']
```

This serializer specifies which fields to include in the serialized representation of **Snippet** instances.

Create a View

Utilize DRF's viewsets or generic views to handle the logic of your API endpoint. For a simple read-only list of snippets, a generic **ListAPIView** can be used:

```
from rest_framework.generics import ListAPIView
from .models import Snippet
from .serializers import SnippetSerializer
class SnippetListView(ListAPIView):
 queryset = Snippet.objects.all()
 serializer_class = SnippetSerializer
```

This view automatically handles GET requests, returning a list of all **Snippet** instances in serialized form.

URL Configuration

Link your API view to a URL. If you haven't done so already, set up a URLconf in your app. Use DRF's **DefaultRouter** for viewsets or include your API views directly for generic views:

```
from django.urls import path
from .views import SnippetListView
urlpatterns = [
 path('snippets/', SnippetListView.as_view(), name='snippet-list'),
]
```

This makes your snippet list API accessible at **/snippets/**, providing a straightforward endpoint for clients to interact with.

To access the endpoint, you just set up, launch your Django development server. You may easily build scalable endpoints that retrieve application data efficiently by creating serializers and using DRF's built-in views. This primary API view for GitforGits code snippet listing improves the platform's functionality and lays the groundwork for future API development, such as endpoints for resource creation, update, and deletion.

Recipe 3: Working with Serializers for Complex

Data

Scenario

In certain cases, nested objects are necessary; for example, when a user has numerous code snippets, each with its own annotations and tags. An in-depth familiarity with DRF serializers is necessary for managing this complicated relational data in APIs. The usability and maintainability of your API, as well as its ability to manage complex data relationships, depend on serializers that are properly constructed.

Desired Solution

Serializers in DRF play a crucial role in converting complex queryset and model instances into JSON and vice versa. They provide a powerful mechanism for dealing with nested data, serialization of multiple objects, and custom fields.

Implementing Nested Serializers

To handle nested objects, define serializers for each level of your data model. For instance, if you have models for User, Snippet, and Comment, create a serializer for each.

```
from rest_framework import serializers

from .models import User, Snippet, Comment

class CommentSerializer(serializers.ModelSerializer):

 class Meta:

 model = Comment

 fields = ('id', 'body', 'author')

class SnippetSerializer(serializers.ModelSerializer):

 comments = CommentSerializer(many=True, read_only=True)

 class Meta:

 model = Snippet
```

```
fields = ('id', 'title', 'code', 'comments')

class UserSerializer(serializers.ModelSerializer):

snippets = SnippetSerializer(many=True, read_only=True)

class Meta:

model = User

fields = ('id', 'username', 'snippets')
```

This setup allows you to serialize a User instance including their snippets and the comments on those snippets, fully representing the nested relationships in your data.

Writing Custom Create and Update Methods

For nested serializers, you may need to override the .create() and .update() methods to properly handle nested data on write operations.

```
class SnippetSerializer(serializers.ModelSerializer):

# Assume we have a field `comments_data` for creating/updating comments

comments_data = CommentSerializer(many=True, write_only=True)

class Meta:

model = Snippet

fields = '__all__'

def create(self, validated_data):

comments_data = validated_data.pop('comments_data')

snippet = Snippet.objects.create(**validated_data)

for comment_data in comments_data:
```

```
Comment.objects.create(snippet=snippet, **comment_data)

return snippet
```

This allows for the creation of a Snippet instance along with its associated Comments in one go, handling the nested data structure efficiently.

Handling Complex Reads and Writes

Use DRF's depth option for read operations if you only need nested representations and not nested writes. For complex writes, as shown above, carefully manage the relationships and data integrity in your custom create and update methods. Mastering nested serializers and custom methods for handling complex data ensures that the application can accommodate a rich feature set while maintaining clarity and integrity in data relationships.

Recipe 4: Implementing Authentication and Permissions in APIs

Scenario

Restricted operations, such as adding, editing, or removing code snippets, should only be executed by authorized users. Also, only the original creator or admin users may change or remove a snippet, among other operations that may necessitate certain permissions.

Desired Solution

Authentication and Permissions in DRF

While authentication verifies the user making the request, permissions establish whether or not the user has the authority to carry out the requested task. Custom permission classes can be applied globally or to specific views, and DRF supports several authentication techniques including OAuth and Token Authentication.

Configuring Authentication

To use token authentication, which assigns a unique token to each user, first add the token authentication scheme to your **settings.py**:

```
REST_FRAMEWORK = {
```

```
'DEFAULT_AUTHENTICATION_CLASSES': [
'rest_framework.authentication.TokenAuthentication',
],
...
}
```

Then, run **python manage.py migrate** to create the necessary database tables for storing tokens. You'll need to generate and assign tokens to your users, which can be done manually via the admin site or programmatically during user registration.

Creating Permission Classes

Define custom permissions for actions like editing or deleting a snippet. Create a new file **permissions.py** in your app directory and define a permission class:

```
from rest_framework import permissions
class IsOwnerOrReadOnly(permissions.BasePermission):
 def has_object_permission(self, request, view, obj):
 if request.method in permissions.SAFE_METHODS:
 return True
 return obj.owner == request.user
```

This permission class allows read-only access to unauthenticated users but restricts write permissions to the object's owner.

Applying Authentication and Permissions to Views

Update your API views to use the configured authentication classes and custom permissions. For DRF's class-based views or viewsets, you can set the **authentication_classes** and **permission_classes** attributes:

```
from rest_framework.authentication import TokenAuthentication
```

```
from .permissions import IsOwnerOrReadOnly

class SnippetDetailView(RetrieveUpdateDestroyAPIView):

    ...

    authentication_classes = [TokenAuthentication]

    permission_classes = [IsOwnerOrReadOnly]
```

Ensure that your snippet model includes an **owner** field that references the user who created it, and adjust view logic accordingly. This setup not only protects user data on GitforGits but also provides a flexible framework for defining complex access control policies tailored to your application's needs.

Recipe 5: Customizing Pagination and Filtering

Scenario

Users may experience information overload as the GitforGits platform's API expands to incorporate a larger dataset of code snippets. It is crucial to create personalized pagination and filtering in order to improve data manageability and user experience. Users can refine their search results by applying filters based on language or creation date, for example, while pagination helps to divide the dataset into more understandable chunks. Both functionalities are built-in to DRF, however you can customize them to fit your application and users' needs better.

Desired Solution

Customizing Pagination

DRF supports several pagination styles, but you can create a custom pagination class to define your own pagination behavior. For example, to implement a pagination style that includes the total number of pages and the current page in the response, extend the **PageNumberPagination** class and set the **page_size** to determine how many items to display per page.

```
from rest_framework.pagination import PageNumberPagination

from rest_framework.response import Response
```

```
class CustomPagination(PageNumberPagination):

page_size = 10

page_size_query_param = 'page_size'

max_page_size = 100


def get_paginated_response(self, data):

return Response({

'links': {

'next': self.get_next_link(),

'previous': self.get_previous_link()

},

'total_pages': self.page.paginator.num_pages,

'current_page': self.page.number,

'page_size': self.page_size,

'results': data

})
```

In your view, specify this custom pagination class in the **pagination_class** attribute.

Implementing Filtering

DRF allows for various filtering backends, but for custom filtering logic, you can override the **get_queryset** method in your view. For instance, to filter code snippets by the programming language, you might include:

```
def get_queryset(self):
 queryset = Snippet.objects.all()
 language = self.request.query_params.get('language', None)
 if language is not None:
 queryset = queryset.filter(language=language)
 return queryset
```

This allows API clients to filter the snippets list by appending a **?language=python** parameter to the URL.

Registering the Custom Components

In your project's settings, register the custom pagination class under the **REST_FRAMEWORK** configuration to apply it globally, or apply it to specific views as needed.

```
REST_FRAMEWORK = {
 ...
 'DEFAULT_PAGINATION_CLASS': 'path.to.CustomPagination',
 ...
}
```

By adjusting the DRF application's pagination and filtering settings, you may make the API respond more closely to GitforGits' and its users' demands. The accessibility and user-friendliness of your API are increased by incorporating tools that make data navigation and filtering easier.

Recipe 6: Best Practices for API Versioning in Django

Scenario

There will inevitably be updates to current endpoints or the introduction of new features. But apps and consumers depending on your API might get disrupted by such changes. To handle these changes with grace, it is essential to implement versioning strategies. This will enable you to iterate on your API without losing backward compatibility. To maintain compatibility with current integrations and make room for future advancements, versioning lets clients choose which version of the API to use.

Desired Solution

Choosing a Versioning Scheme

DRF supports various versioning schemes out of the box, including URL path versioning, query parameter versioning, and header versioning. The choice of scheme depends on your API's specific needs and the preferences of its consumers. URL path versioning (**/api/v1/**) is one of the most straightforward and commonly used methods, offering clear and explicit versioning.

Configuring Versioning in DRF

To set up URL path versioning in your project, update the **DEFAULT_VERSIONING_CLASS** in your **settings.py** to use **rest_framework.versioning.URLPathVersioning**. Also, specify a default version and allowed versions:

```
REST_FRAMEWORK = {

 'DEFAULT_VERSIONING_CLASS':
'rest_framework.versioning.URLPathVersioning',

 'DEFAULT_VERSION': 'v1',

 'ALLOWED_VERSIONS': ['v1', 'v2'],

 'VERSION_PARAM': 'version',

}
```

Adapting Your URLs and Views

Modify your **urls.py** to include the version in the URL path. DRF's **path** function supports versioning directly:

```
from django.urls import path, include
```

```
from rest_framework.routers import DefaultRouter

from . import views

# Assuming you have a router set up for your views

router = DefaultRouter()

router.register(r'snippets', views.SnippetViewSet)

urlpatterns = [

 path('api/<version>/', include(router.urls)),

]
```

In your views, you can access the version of the request via **request.version** and adjust the behavior accordingly.

Communicating Changes and Deprecations

Clearly document available versions, changes in each version, and any deprecated features or endpoints. Communication with your API consumers is key to a smooth transition between versions. Consider providing migration guides or examples to help users adapt to new versions.

Deprecation Policy

Establish a deprecation policy outlining how long old versions will be supported. This policy helps manage expectations and provides a clear timeline for transitioning between API versions.

Recipe 7: Testing DRF Applications

Scenario

Testing is essential in the development cycle since it helps to detect defects, prevent regressions, and ensure that the API fits its design standards. You can significantly improve the stability and dependability of your API by implementing a thorough testing approach that includes unit tests for specific components and integration tests for endpoints.

Desired Solution

Setting Up the Test Environment

Configure your Django project to use a separate database for testing to avoid interfering with your development data. This can typically be done in your project's **settings.py** by customizing the **DATABASES** setting when **TEST** is in the environment variables.

Testing DRF Views

DRF includes a **APIClient** class, extending Django's **Client** test class, that simulates requests to the API and is aware of things like authentication.

```
from rest_framework.test import APIClient

from django.urls import reverse

from rest_framework import status

import pytest

@pytest.mark.django_db

def test_snippet_list():

 client = APIClient()

 url = reverse('snippet-list')

 response = client.get(url)

 assert response.status_code == status.HTTP_200_OK
```

The above sample program tests that the snippet list view returns a 200 OK response, indicating it is accessible as expected.

Testing Authentication and Permissions

Use the **force_authenticate** method with the **APIClient** to simulate authenticated requests in your tests.

```
from django.contrib.auth.models import User

from rest_framework.test import APIClient
```

```
from .models import Snippet

def test_create_snippet_authenticated():

 client = APIClient()

 user = User.objects.create_user('testuser', 'test@gitforgits.com', 'testpassword')

 client.force_authenticate(user=user)

 url = reverse('snippet-list')

 data = {'title': 'Test Snippet', 'code': 'print("hello, world")'}

 response = client.post(url, data, format='json')

 assert response.status_code == status.HTTP_201_CREATED
```

This test ensures authenticated users can create snippets.

Integration Testing

Beyond individual unit tests, consider writing integration tests that test the API's workflow from end to end. These tests can simulate a user's interaction with multiple endpoints and validate the overall functionality and performance of your API.

Continuous Integration

Integrate your tests into a CI/CD pipeline to automatically run them against every commit or pull request. This practice helps identify issues early and improves code quality.

Through a combination of unit and integration tests, you can cover a wide range of scenarios, ensuring that your API functions correctly under various conditions and adheres to its specified behavior.

Recipe 8: Debugging DRF Applications

Scenario

If you want to keep your service up and running smoothly, find and fix problems fast, and keep your users happy, you need debugging tactics that work. The interplay between serializers, views, authentication systems, and third-party clients in DRF applications, like in any complex system, can make debugging a unique difficulty.

Desired Solution

Leveraging DRF's Browsable API

One of DRF's most powerful features for development and debugging is its browsable API interface. It not only provides a human-friendly way to interact with your API but also displays useful debugging information such as request and response data, status codes, and headers. When encountering an issue, first use the browsable API to replicate the problem and observe any errors or unexpected output.

Django Debug Toolbar

The Django Debug Toolbar is an invaluable tool for debugging Django applications, including those using DRF. It offers detailed insights into the SQL queries generated by your views, performance data, request and response headers, and more. To use it with DRF, ensure your API views are capable of rendering HTML responses or temporarily switch to a standard Django view while debugging.

```
INSTALLED_APPS += ['debug_toolbar']

MIDDLEWARE += ['debug_toolbar.middleware.DebugToolbarMiddleware']

DEBUG_TOOLBAR_CONFIG = {

 'SHOW_TOOLBAR_CALLBACK': lambda request: True, # Forces the toolbar to
show for DRF views

}
```

Logging

Properly configured logging can provide insights into your application's behavior, capturing detailed information about requests, responses, and system errors. Django's logging framework is highly configurable, allowing you to log messages at various severity levels and output logs to different destinations (console, file, email, etc.).

```
LOGGING = {

 'version': 1,
```

```
'disable_existing_loggers': False,
'handlers': {
'console': {
'class': 'logging.StreamHandler',
},
},
'loggers': {
'django': {
'handlers': ['console'],
'level': 'DEBUG',
},
},
}
```

Postman and cURL for Testing API Calls

Tools like Postman or cURL can simulate client requests to your API, offering a way to methodically test and debug various API endpoints. They are particularly useful for debugging authentication issues, testing header configurations, and replicating client-reported errors.

DRF's Exception Handling

Customize DRF's exception handling to catch and log exceptions or to modify the response data for errors. DRF provides hooks for custom exception handling, which can be used to add debugging information to error responses or integrate with error tracking services.

Recipe 9: Implementing Throttling and Rate Limiting for APIs

Scenario

The GitforGits API starts to see a dramatic spike in traffic as the platform becomes more popular. All users may experience decreased performance or availability as a result of resource pressure caused by this surge. It is necessary to apply throttle and rate restriction in order to maintain a high level of service and ensure equitable usage. These safeguards protect the system from possible misuse and overuse by preventing any one user or client from making excessive requests.

Desired Solution

Understanding Throttling in DRF

Throttling in DRF allows you to define limits on how often a user can make requests to your API within a given timeframe. These limits can be applied globally or to individual views, and DRF includes several throttling classes to suit different use cases.

Configure Throttling Settings

To implement throttling, start by specifying the desired throttling classes and rates in your project's **settings.py**. DRF provides **SimpleRateThrottle** for basic use cases, and you can define custom rates:

```
REST_FRAMEWORK = {
 'DEFAULT_THROTTLE_CLASSES': [
 'rest_framework.throttling.AnonRateThrottle',
 'rest_framework.throttling.UserRateThrottle'
 ],
 'DEFAULT_THROTTLE_RATES': {
 'anon': '100/day',
 'user': '1000/day'
 }
}
```

This configuration sets a rate limit of 100 requests per day for unauthenticated users and 1,000 for authenticated users.

Creating Custom Throttle Classes

For more complex scenarios, you can create custom throttle classes by subclassing **BaseThrottle**. This is particularly useful for implementing rate limits based on criteria other than user identity or IP address, such as endpoint-specific throttling:

```
from rest_framework.throttling import SimpleRateThrottle

class SnippetCreateThrottle(SimpleRateThrottle):

 scope = 'snippet_create'

 def get_cache_key(self, request, view):

 if request.method == 'POST':

 return request.user.id

 return None
```

Then, add **'snippet_create': '10/hour'** to **DEFAULT_THROTTLE_RATES** and apply your custom throttle to specific views.

Applying Throttling to Views

Throttling can be applied to views by setting the **throttle_classes** attribute. For class-based views or viewsets, you can directly specify which throttling classes to use:

```
from rest_framework.throttling import UserRateThrottle

from .throttling import SnippetCreateThrottle

class SnippetListView(ListCreateAPIView):

 throttle_classes = [UserRateThrottle, SnippetCreateThrottle]

 # View setup continues...
```

Handling Throttling Responses

When a request exceeds the defined rate limits, DRF will return a 429 Too Many Requests response. Customize the response or inform users about the throttling policy through documentation and API error messages.

By regulating the maximum request rate, you may prevent the GitforGits platform from being overloaded and make sure that everyone has an equal chance to use the resources, which will improve the platform for everyone and make it more stable.

Summary

To help developers turn GitforGits into an interactive platform, this chapter provides an extensive set of recipes for using DRF to build, test, and manage powerful APIs. Beginning with the basics of getting DRF up and running, this chapter introduces best practices for organizing and configuring DRF inside a Django project, laying the framework for API development. An important next step in the process is building the first API view; this will show how easy and powerful DRF is for making application data accessible through web APIs. In order to facilitate data interchange between servers and clients, the recipe builds upon the previously covered recipe by exploring serializers for complicated data and showing how to effectively convert Django models into JSON or XML forms.

Later, the chapter dives into more complex issues including API versioning best practices, modifying pagination and filtering, and establishing authentication and permissions. By demonstrating several methods for protecting APIs, controlling access, and improving the user experience with personalized data presentation and navigation, these recipes showcase the richness and flexibility of DRF. Developers can find techniques to make sure their APIs work properly in different situations in the recipe on testing and debugging DRF apps, which highlights the significance of dependability and robustness in API development. To further secure the application from misuse and guarantee fair distribution of resources across users, throttle and rate restriction can be applied to handle the operational parts of API management.

In sum, developers are going to finish this chapter with the technical know-how to fully utilize DRF and a firm grasp of the concepts underpinning RESTful API management and design. This chapter teaches developers how to construct APIs that are efficient, secure, and scalable by combining recipes on DRF's features with advice on best practices for API creation.

CHAPTER 8: TESTING, SECURITY, AND DEPLOYMENT

Introduction

This chapter is designed to help you through the last and most important steps of constructing a Django application. It focuses on making sure your project is secure, has high quality, and can be deployed successfully, similar to GitforGits. The chapter highlights the significance of careful testing, strong security measures, and easy deployment procedures. From doing preliminary unit tests to securely deploying your application, each recipe in this chapter covers a key component of getting your Django application ready for real-world use.

In the first recipe, "Writing Unit Tests in Django," you will find the necessary skills to create and execute tests that validate your application's functionality and behavior. This will help you avoid regressions caused by modifications to the code. A high-quality codebase cannot be maintained without this basis. Carrying this notion further, Automate Testing in Django focuses into the ins and outs of establishing automated testing environments to improve the development workflow, find issues earlier, and make tests a crucial component of the development cycle.

As we approach the deployment phase, If you want to set up a server environment that is perfect for Django apps, then you ought to check out the recipe 'Setting up a Production Environment for Django Apps'. It will help you establish the groundwork for a successful deployment. Next, you'll learn how to move your Django app from a development environment to production servers by following the instructions in Deploying Django Applications to Production. This includes setting up web servers, WSGI applications, and dealing with dynamic content. Assuring the timeliness and reliability of your application relies on efficiently serving static material in a production scenario. This is where Managing Static Files in Production Environments comes in.

To prevent unauthorized parties from intercepting or altering critical data, it is crucial to implement secure communications between your application and its users. This can be achieved from the recipe 'HTTPS and SSL certificates'. Especially for apps that deal with sensitive financial or personal data, this recipe is crucial for gaining users' trust. The chapter concludes with an introduction to the ideas and tools needed to set up continuous integration and continuous deployment pipelines for Django apps. These pipelines automate the process from code changes to testing and deployment, making the road to production much smoother.

Recipe 1: Writing Unit Tests in Django

Scenario

As time goes on, it becomes more important to make sure its features are stable and reliable. As a means to methodically check that specific parts work as intended, unit testing becomes an essential part of this guarantee. A built-in Python library for implementing unit tests, the unittest module makes it easy to write unit tests in Django. To make sure that the application works as expected in different situations, this module lets developers create test cases that are separate from each other, repeatable, and not affected by outside influences.

Desired Solution

Overview of the `unittest` *Module*

The unittest module provides a rich set of tools for constructing and running tests. It supports test automation, sharing of setup and shutdown code for tests, aggregation of tests into collections, and independence of the tests from the reporting framework. The basic building blocks of a unit test in Django are test cases, which are Python classes that inherit from unittest.TestCase.

Setting Up Your Test Environment

Django looks for tests in any file named with a test prefix. Create a file named test_models.py in your application's tests directory to test your models. Ensure your Django settings use a separate database for testing to avoid interfering with your development data.

Writing a Unit Test for a Django Model

Suppose you have a Snippet model in your application that you want to test. You aim to verify that creating and saving a new Snippet instance works as expected.

```
from django.test import TestCase

from .models import Snippet

class SnippetModelTest(TestCase):

 def setUp(self):

 # Setup run before every test method.

 Snippet.objects.create(title="Hello World", code="print('Hello, world!')")

 def test_snippet_content(self):

 # Test retrieving a snippet and verifying its content.

 snippet = Snippet.objects.get(title="Hello World")

 expected_object_name = f'{snippet.title}'
```

```
expected_object_code = f'{snippet.code}'

self.assertEqual(expected_object_name, "Hello World")

self.assertEqual(expected_object_code, "print('Hello, world!')")
```

This test case SnippetModelTest contains two test methods: setUp, which initializes a Snippet instance before each test, and test_snippet_content, which asserts that the snippet's title and code are correctly stored and retrieved.

Running the Tests

Execute your tests by running the following command:

```
python manage.py test
```

Django will discover tests under any file named with a tests.py pattern or files in a tests directory and execute them using the unittest framework.

Analyzing Test Results

Django prints the results to the console after each test run, letting you know if the tests succeeded or failed. When Django encounters an error, it produces comprehensive output that assists in identifying the cause of the problem. Developers may build a more solid and reliable platform by thoroughly testing each component to find and fix bugs faster. In order to ensure that the application continues to be manageable and free of errors, this recipe establishes the groundwork for a strong testing approach in GitforGits.

Recipe 2: Automate Testing in Django

Scenario

Running tests manually becomes tedious and error-prone as the set of unit tests for GitforGits grows. Particularly prior to integrating new code into the main codebase, automation is crucial for guaranteeing consistent execution of tests. Streamline development workflows, detect regressions rapidly, and maintain excellent code quality by automating your Django testing process. You may achieve continuous testing across the whole development lifecycle by including automated testing into your pipelines for development and deployment.

Desired Solution

Integrating with Version Control Hooks

Use pre-commit hooks in your version control system (e.g., Git) to run tests automatically before each commit. This ensures that all changes pass your test suite before they can be added to the repository. For Git, you can configure a pre-commit hook in the .git/hooks/pre-commit file of your repository:

```
#!/bin/sh

python manage.py test

if [ $? -ne 0 ]; then

 echo "Tests failed, aborting commit."

 exit 1

fi
```

Make sure to make this script executable with chmod +x .git/hooks/pre-commit.

Continuous Integration (CI) Services

Continuous Integration services such as GitHub Actions, GitLab CI/CD, or Jenkins can be configured to automatically run your test suite on various events, like pushing to a repository or creating a pull request. For instance, setting up a GitHub Actions workflow involves creating a .github/workflows/django-ci.yml file in your repository with the following content:

```
name: Django CI

on: [push, pull_request]

jobs:

 build:

 runs-on: ubuntu-latest

 steps:

 - uses: actions/checkout@v2
```

```
- name: Set up Python

uses: actions/setup-python@v2

with:

python-version: '3.8'

- name: Install dependencies

run: |

python -m pip install --upgrade pip

pip install -r requirements.txt

- name: Run tests

run: python manage.py test
```

This workflow installs your project's dependencies and runs your Django test suite every time code is pushed to your repository or a pull request is made.

Automated Test Reporting

Enhance feedback from automated testing by integrating test reporting tools that provide detailed insights and alerts on test outcomes. Many CI services offer built-in test reporting features or can be integrated with third-party services like TestRail, Allure, or Codecov for more comprehensive reporting.

Recipe 3: Setting up Production Environment for Django Apps

Scenario

To make sure GitforGits is secure, scalable, and performs effectively under different loads, you need to put up a production environment before you can take it live. Your Django application will be deployed on Amazon Web Services (AWS), namely on Elastic Compute Cloud (EC2), Relational Database Service (RDS), and Simple Storage Service (S3), due to the abundance of alternatives available. To facilitate communication between your program and the web, Gunicorn will act as the WSGI HTTP server. This recipe provides a step-by-step solution on how to use these technologies to get your Django application ready for production on AWS.

Desired Solution

AWS Setup

- EC2 Instance: Start by launching an EC2 instance using the AWS Management Console. Choose an AMI that comes with Ubuntu, as it is widely supported and documented.
- RDS Database: Set up an RDS instance for your database, selecting PostgreSQL. Ensure it is in the same VPC as your EC2 instance for seamless connectivity. Secure your RDS instance by allowing access only from your EC2 instance's security group.
- S3 Buckets: Create two S3 buckets through the AWS Console, one for static files and another for media files. Configure the buckets for public access since they'll serve your application's assets directly.

EC2 Instance Configuration

- SSH into your EC2 instance after its setup.
- Update the package list and install Python, pip, and virtualenv:

```
sudo apt-get update

sudo apt-get install python3-pip python3-dev libpq-dev nginx git

sudo -H pip3 install --upgrade pip

sudo -H pip3 install virtualenv
```

- Create a directory for your project and set up a virtual environment within this directory. Activate it and install Django, Gunicorn, psycopg2 (PostgreSQL adapter), and django-storages.
- Clone your GitforGits repository into this directory or upload your project files.

Database Configuration

Update your Django project's settings.py to use the RDS instance. Configure the DATABASES setting with your RDS endpoint, database name, user, and password.

Static and Media Files Configuration

- In settings.py, configure django-storages to use S3 buckets for static and media files. Set STATIC_URL, STATIC_ROOT, MEDIA_URL, and MEDIA_ROOT to point to your S3 buckets.
- Ensure you have the necessary IAM permissions and that your AWS credentials are securely configured.

Gunicorn Configuration

- Inside your virtual environment, run Gunicorn to test it is working with your project:

```
gunicorn --workers 3 your_project.wsgi:application
```

- Create a systemd service file for Gunicorn to ensure it starts at boot and restarts on failure. Configure it to point to your project's WSGI module.

Nginx Configuration

Set up Nginx as a reverse proxy to forward requests to Gunicorn. Configure Nginx by creating a new site configuration in /etc/nginx/sites-available/ and link it to sites-enabled. The configuration should include the location of your static files and proxy_pass directives for your Gunicorn server.

Securing Your Application

- Implement HTTPS by obtaining an SSL certificate with Let's Encrypt or AWS Certificate Manager. Configure Nginx to use the SSL certificate, redirecting all HTTP traffic to HTTPS.
- Restart Nginx and start the Gunicorn service via systemd.
- Ensure your EC2 instance's security group allows traffic on port 80 (HTTP) and 443 (HTTPS).

By following this recipe, GitforGits our any application is now ready to serve its users reliably on AWS with a robust infrastructure in place, ensuring a smooth and scalable application experience.

Recipe 4: Deploying Django Applications to Production

Scenario

With the following prerequisites met: a running AWS EC2 instance, database RDS configuration, static and media file S3 setup, Gunicorn installation and testing, and reverse proxy Nginx configuration, you are nearly ready to go live. You should commit and push your local modifications to your repository if you are using a version control system (VCS) like Git.

Desired Solution

Update Your Code

- SSH into your EC2 instance.
- Navigate to your project directory where you've cloned your GitforGits repository.
- Pull the latest changes from your repository or upload the updated project files directly.

Activate Your Virtual Environment

Ensure your virtual environment is activated before proceeding with the next steps.

```
source venv/bin/activate
```

Install Dependencies

Install or update any new dependencies in your virtual environment specified in your requirements.txt.

```
pip install -r requirements.txt
```

Run Migrations

Apply any new migrations to your RDS database instance.

```
python manage.py migrate
```

Collect Static Files

Run the collectstatic command to upload all static files to your configured S3 bucket.

```
python manage.py collectstatic
```

This step ensures that your static assets are updated and available through S3.

Check for Errors

Before restarting your application server, run the Django check command to identify any system checks that fail.

```
python manage.py check --deploy
```

Restart Gunicorn

Restart the Gunicorn service to apply the new changes. If you've set up Gunicorn as a systemd service, use:

```
sudo systemctl restart gunicorn
```

This ensures Gunicorn is running with the latest version of your application.

Verify Nginx Configuration

- Ensure Nginx is properly configured to serve your application, especially if there have been changes to domain names, SSL certificates, or if adding HTTP2 support.
- Test the Nginx configuration for syntax errors:

```
sudo nginx -t
```

- Reload Nginx to apply any changes:

```
sudo systemctl reload nginx
```

Then, ensure all firewall rules, security groups in AWS, and database permissions are correctly set to only allow necessary traffic and connections. And, do not forget to set up monitoring and logging tools (e.g., AWS CloudWatch, Sentry for Django) to track application performance and errors in real-time.

Recipe 5: Managing Static Files in Production

Scenario

Now that your Django app is live on AWS and providing dynamic content via Nginx and Gunicorn, it is critical to manage static files efficiently in a production setting. While it is great that Django takes care of serving static files (CSS, JavaScript, pictures) while you are developing, it is recommended to use a dedicated web server or a cloud storage service when you are in production. Based on the configuration in the previous recipes, a strong solution is to use AWS S3 to store static files and Nginx to serve them. This will ensure fast load times and reduce the strain on your application server.

Desired Solution

Setting Up AWS S3 for Static Files

- Create a new S3 bucket through the AWS Management Console specifically for your static files. Ensure the bucket is publicly accessible and set up CORS (Cross-Origin Resource Sharing) if your application requires accessing these files from different domains.
- Install django-storages and boto3 via pip to integrate S3 with your Django project:

```
pip install django-storages boto3
```

- Add 'storages' to your INSTALLED_APPS in settings.py and configure the static files settings to use S3:

```
AWS_ACCESS_KEY_ID = 'your-access-key'

AWS_SECRET_ACCESS_KEY = 'your-secret-key'

AWS_STORAGE_BUCKET_NAME = 'your-bucket-name'

AWS_S3_CUSTOM_DOMAIN =
f'{AWS_STORAGE_BUCKET_NAME}.s3.amazonaws.com'

AWS_S3_OBJECT_PARAMETERS = {'CacheControl': 'max-age=86400'}

# static files

STATIC_URL = f'https://{AWS_S3_CUSTOM_DOMAIN}/static/'

STATICFILES_STORAGE = 'storages.backends.s3boto3.S3Boto3Storage'
```

- Run python manage.py collectstatic to upload your static files to the configured S3 bucket.

Nginx as a Reverse Proxy for Static Files

While serving static files directly from S3 is efficient, using Nginx as a reverse proxy can offer benefits such as caching, compression, and logging. This setup involves configuring Nginx to first look for static files in a local directory (which acts as a cache) and then proxy requests to S3 if the file isn't found locally.

Configure an Nginx server block to handle static files

```
server {
 listen 80;
 server_name yourdomain.com;
 location /static/ {
 proxy_pass https://your-bucket-name.s3.amazonaws.com/static/;
 proxy_set_header Host your-bucket-name.s3.amazonaws.com;
 proxy_cache mycache;
 proxy_cache_valid 200 1d;
 add_header Cache-Control "public";
 }
}
```

Ensure you have a caching mechanism configured in Nginx to minimize the requests to S3 and improve response times for static files.

Testing

After configuring S3 and updating Nginx, test loading your application's static assets to ensure they are being served correctly and efficiently from S3 through Nginx.

Use tools like Google PageSpeed Insights to measure the performance impact of your static file serving setup and make adjustments as needed.

A scalable and efficient solution for GitforGits may be achieved by using AWS S3 for storage and Nginx for providing static content. This ensures that users will reliably and rapidly receive their static assets.

Recipe 6: Implementing HTTPS and SSL Certificates

Scenario

With a powerful combination of Nginx and Gunicorn, your GitforGits Django application is now up and running on AWS, ready to serve users. But right now, the app is serving traffic over the unsafe HTTP protocol. Users must move to HTTPS in order to protect their data, particularly their login passwords and personal details. An excellent option for application security is Let's Encrypt, which provides a free and automated approach to obtain SSL/TLS certificates.

Desired Solution

Obtain a Domain Name

Ensure you have a registered domain name pointing to your AWS EC2 instance. Update your domain's DNS settings to create an A record that points to the public IP address of your EC2 instance.

Install Certbot

Certbot is a free tool that automates the process of obtaining and renewing Let's Encrypt certificates. Install Certbot and its Nginx plugin on your EC2 instance:

```
sudo apt-get update

sudo apt-get install certbot python3-certbot-nginx
```

Obtaining the Certificate

Run Certbot with the Nginx plugin to automatically configure SSL for Nginx and obtain a certificate:

```
sudo certbot --nginx -d yourdomain.com -d www.yourdomain.com
```

Follow the prompts to complete the process. Certbot will modify your Nginx configuration to use the obtained SSL certificate and set up automatic renewals.

Configuring Nginx for HTTPS

Certbot usually handles the necessary configuration changes, but you can verify or adjust the settings in your Nginx site configuration *(/etc/nginx/sites-available/yourdomain.com):*

```
server {
 listen 80;
 server_name yourdomain.com www.yourdomain.com;
 return 301 https://$server_name$request_uri;
}
server {
 listen 443 ssl http2;
 server_name yourdomain.com www.yourdomain.com;
 ssl_certificate /etc/letsencrypt/live/yourdomain.com/fullchain.pem;
 ssl_certificate_key /etc/letsencrypt/live/yourdomain.com/privkey.pem;
 # Further SSL settings and server configuration
}
```

This setup redirects all HTTP traffic to HTTPS and enables HTTP/2 for improved performance.

Testing Your Configuration

Check your Nginx configuration for syntax errors:

```
sudo nginx -t
```

Reload Nginx to apply the changes:

```
sudo systemctl reload nginx
```

Automatic Renewal

Let's Encrypt certificates are valid for 90 days. Certbot creates a cron job or systemd timer to automatically renew certificates before they expire. Ensure this automation is in place and working:

```
sudo certbot renew --dry-run
```

Your site's trustworthiness and search engine ranking will both be enhanced, and sensitive data will be protected, by doing this. Keep an eye on the dates of your SSL setup and certificate expiration to make sure your HTTPS service remains uninterrupted.

Summary

In sum, moving Django apps from the development to production environment was made much easier by following the steps outlined in this chapter. Prior to delving into the specifics of writing and automating unit tests in Django's, this chapter stressed the significance of thorough testing. For early issue detection, code quality assurance, and regression prevention, testing is crucial. Continuous integration and delivery (CI/CD) procedures enable the automated testing and efficient deployment of code changes, significantly streamlining the development process. This method cuts down on wasted time and human mistake by a large margin.

The chapter continued with demonstrating how to get a Django app ready for production. The recipe went over everything from configuring an AWS production environment to efficient file management with AWS S3, application deployment with Gunicorn and Nginx, and more. Ensuring encrypted communication between the server and its clients, security was a top priority when developing this online application. HTTPS and SSL certificates were used to accomplish this. From optimizing web server and database configurations to safeguarding the application against any threats, the deployment process was extremely extensive. Last but not least, the chapter covered the suggested techniques for setting up CI/CD pipelines, which help applications streamline their workflow during development, testing, and deployment.

CHAPTER 9: ADVANCED WEB APPLICATION FEATURES WITH DJANGO

Introduction

This chapter is designed to improve the app's capabilities by introducing a series of sophisticated functionalities that take advantage of Django's adaptability and robustness. This chapter goes beyond the fundamentals, delving into more complicated web application features that improve interactivity, personalization, and performance.

Beginning with Implementing Advanced AJAX in Django, we will look into AJAX techniques for creating extremely responsive and dynamic user interfaces. This recipe focuses on improving client-server communication, allowing the application to update information and respond to user activities in real time without having to reload the whole page. Next, Creating and Managing Custom User Profiles deals with personalization by extending the normal user model. This strategy makes it easier to acquire, store, and manipulate extra user information, allowing you to personalize your user experience to your specific tastes and activities.

Generating Dynamic Content with Django Templates gets into how Django's templating engine can generate HTML content dynamically based on context and user data. This functionality is critical for delivering tailored content to users and improving their connection with the platform. For better code reuse and maintainability, Building Custom Decorators for Views provides a way to standardize the implementation of common behaviors and patterns across many views, including logging or access restrictions.

Recipes such as Implementing Real-time Features with Django Channels and Implementing WebSockets in Your Django Application teach developers the process of incorporating WebSockets for bidirectional communication between client and server. Because of this, additional features can be created to enhance the user experience, such as live notifications, chat systems, and real-time updates.

Finally, Performing Efficient Full-text Search with Django addresses the difficulty of building a robust and efficient search system. This recipe uses Django's built-in features and external tools to allow users to do quick, relevant searches across the application's data, hence boosting content accessibility and discovery.

In sum, this chapter 9 provides developers with the tools and expertise they need to implement complicated, current features into their Django applications, pushing the framework's capabilities.

Recipe 1: Implementing Advanced AJAX in Django

Scenario

One of our primary objectives is to improve the user experience by introducing a more dynamic and responsive interface that does not require complete page refreshes. With AJAX, web pages can have their content updated in response to events or user activities, giving the impression that applications are more responsive and lively. Features like live search, form validation, and content updates can be implemented with the help of powerful AJAX functionalities, allowing users to have a smoother platform interaction with an instant response.

Desired Solution

Setting Up

Ensure you have jQuery or a similar JavaScript library/framework integrated into your Django project for ease of handling AJAX requests, though you can also use vanilla JavaScript's **XMLHttpRequest** or the Fetch API.

Create a Django view dedicated to handling AJAX requests. This view should return JSON responses, which can be dynamically inserted into your templates.

Creating an AJAX-enabled Django View

Suppose you want to implement a live search feature that updates search results as the user types. First, create a view that filters your model based on the search query received via an AJAX request.

```
from django.http import JsonResponse

from .models import Snippet

def search_snippets(request):

 if request.is_ajax():

 query = request.GET.get('q', '')

 snippets = Snippet.objects.filter(title__icontains=query).values('title', 'code')[:5]

 return JsonResponse(list(snippets), safe=False)

 return JsonResponse({"error": "AJAX request required."}, status=400)
```

This view expects an AJAX request with a query parameter **q** and returns a JSON response containing up to 5 snippets matching the search query.

AJAX Request in the Template

In your template, add a search input field and a container where search results will be displayed.

Then, write JavaScript to handle the input event of the search field, sending an AJAX request to your Django view and displaying the results.

```
<input type="text" id="searchQuery" placeholder="Search snippets...">

<div id="searchResults"></div>

<script>

$('#searchQuery').on('input', function() {

 $.ajax({

 url: '/search_snippets/',

 data: { 'q': $(this).val() },

 dataType: 'json',

 success: function(data) {

 $('#searchResults').empty();

 $.each(data, function(index, snippet) {

 $('#searchResults').append($('<div>').text(snippet.title));

 });

 }

 });

});

</script>
```

This script captures input events on the search field, sends the input value as a query to the server, and updates the **#searchResults** div with the titles of the found snippets.

Security Considerations

- Ensure CSRF tokens are correctly handled if making POST requests. For GET requests (like search), CSRF protection isn't required, but always validate and sanitize inputs on the server to prevent injection attacks.

Rate limit AJAX endpoints to prevent abuse.

This recipe for a live search feature showcases the power of AJAX in creating fluid, app-like interfaces within GitforGits, encouraging user engagement and satisfaction.

Recipe 2: Creating and Managing Custom User Profiles

Scenario

While Django's basic user model can manage authentication, it may lack some of the fields that are essential to your application's functionality. Additional information like a user's bio, profile picture, or social media profile links could be useful when personalization and engagement are priorities. You can collect and use this extra data all over your app by making a user profile model that is an extension of the default user model.

Desired Solution

Define a Custom User Profile Model

Extend Django's built-in **User** model by creating a one-to-one link to a custom **UserProfile** model that contains the additional fields.

```
from django.db import models

from django.contrib.auth.models import User

from django.db.models.signals import post_save

from django.dispatch import receiver

class UserProfile(models.Model):

 user = models.OneToOneField(User, on_delete=models.CASCADE)

 bio = models.TextField(max_length=500, blank=True)
```

```
profile_picture = models.ImageField(upload_to='profile_pics/', null=True,
blank=True)

website_url = models.URLField(blank=True, null=True)

def __str__(self):

return self.user.username
```

Automatically Create User Profile

Use Django signals to automatically create a **UserProfile** instance whenever a new **User** is created. This ensures that each user has an associated profile.

```
@receiver(post_save, sender=User)

def create_user_profile(sender, instance, created, **kwargs):

if created:

UserProfile.objects.create(user=instance)

@receiver(post_save, sender=User)

def save_user_profile(sender, instance, **kwargs):

instance.userprofile.save()
```

Integrate Custom User Profile into Admin:

To manage user profiles easily, integrate the **UserProfile** model into Django's admin. This allows for viewing and editing profile information directly from the admin interface.

```
from django.contrib import admin

from .models import UserProfile

class UserProfileAdmin(admin.ModelAdmin):

list_display = ('user', 'bio', 'website_url')
```

```
admin.site.register(UserProfile, UserProfileAdmin)
```

Updating Views and Templates

Modify your views and templates to include user profile information. For instance, you can allow users to edit their profiles through a form that interacts with the **UserProfile** model.

Ensure your templates display the additional profile information where relevant, enhancing the personalization of the user experience.

Handling Profile Pictures

If using profile pictures, configure your media files settings and ensure your production server is properly set up to serve these files, similar to how static files are managed.

Your application's personalization and functionality can be significantly improved using Django's custom user profiles. This method not only creates a more personalized experience for users by letting them disclose more about themselves, but it also sets the framework for features that use user profile information to make your app more interesting.

Recipe 3: Generating Dynamic Content using Django Templates

Scenario

For instance, the homepage could include personalized welcome messages or suggestions, or an administrator logging in might see different alternatives than an ordinary user. By utilizing template tags, filters, and inheritance, Let us see if Django templates can provide means of displaying such dynamic content with its robust templating engine.

Desired Solution

Understanding Django Template System

Django's templating system uses tags ({% %}) and filters ({{ }}) to inject dynamic content into HTML. It is designed to separate the presentation of data from the logic that generates the data, making your templates easier to maintain.

Using Template Tags and Filters

To display personalized greetings based on the time of day, you can use template tags in your template:

```
{% if user.is_authenticated %}

<p>Good {{ greeting }}, {{ user.username }}!</p>

{% endif %}
```

In your view, add logic to determine the part of the day and pass it as context to the template:

```
from django.shortcuts import render

import datetime

def home(request):

 current_hour = datetime.datetime.now().hour

 if current_hour < 12:

 greeting = "morning"

 elif 12 <= current_hour < 18:

 greeting = "afternoon"

 else:

 greeting = "evening"

 context = {'greeting': greeting}

 return render(request, 'home.html', context)
```

Incorporating Template Inheritance

Use template inheritance to maintain a consistent layout across your application while injecting dynamic content where needed. Create a base template (**base.html**) that defines blocks that child templates can override:

```
<!-- base.html -->

<!DOCTYPE html>
```

```
<html>
<head>
 <title>{% block title %}GitforGits{% endblock %}</title>
</head>
<body>
 {% block content %}
 {% endblock %}
</body>
</html>
```

Child templates extend the base template and fill in the content block with dynamic content:

```
{% extends 'base.html' %}


{% block content %}
 <p>This is a dynamic message for the user.</p>
{% endblock %}
```

Leveraging Template Context Processors

For content that needs to be dynamically generated across many pages, consider using a context processor. It allows you to inject dynamic content into the context of every template across your application.

Create a custom context processor that adds data to the template context:

```
def add_custom_data(request):
 return {'site_name': 'GitforGits'}
```

Add your context processor to the **TEMPLATES** setting in **settings.py**. This approach allows for the seamless integration of variable content based on user actions, preferences, or any other context-specific data, enhancing engagement and the overall usability of the platform.

Recipe 4: Building Custom Decorators for Views

Scenario

Consistently applying the same checks or procedures to different views is becoming more laborious. Take the following example: you may like to restrict editing and deleting of snippets to only those who have written them. Alternatively, you may wish to record who has accessed which views for auditing reasons. You may make your views more consistent and clean with the help of Python decorators, which provide a strong approach to encapsulate and reuse common functionality. Without cluttering your views with boilerplate code, you can elegantly encapsulate functionality around your view logic by creating custom decorators for your Django views. This allows you to enforce rules or enhance their behavior.

Desired Solution

Creating a Custom Decorator

A decorator is a function that takes another function as an argument and extends its behavior without explicitly modifying it. In Django, decorators are extensively used for view logic, like requiring login for access to a particular view.

Suppose you want to create a decorator that ensures only the author of a snippet can edit or delete it. You can create a decorator that checks this condition and either proceeds with the view or redirects the user with an error message.

```
from django.http import HttpResponseForbidden

from django.shortcuts import get_object_or_404, redirect

from .models import Snippet

def user_is_snippet_author(view_func):

 def _wrapped_view_func(request, *args, **kwargs):

 snippet = get_object_or_404(Snippet, pk=kwargs['pk'])
```

```
if snippet.author != request.user:

return HttpResponseForbidden()

return view_func(request, *args, **kwargs)

return _wrapped_view_func
```

This decorator first retrieves the snippet based on the **pk** argument expected in the view's keyword arguments. It then checks if the current user is the author of the snippet. If not, it returns a **HttpResponseForbidden**, otherwise, it proceeds with the original view function.

Applying the Decorator to Views

To apply your custom decorator, simply wrap your view functions with it. For class-based views, you'll need to use the **method_decorator** helper.

```
from django.utils.decorators import method_decorator

from django.views.generic import UpdateView

from .models import Snippet

from .decorators import user_is_snippet_author

@method_decorator(user_is_snippet_author, name='dispatch')

class SnippetUpdateView(UpdateView):

model = Snippet

fields = ['title', 'code']

template_name = 'snippets/edit.html'
```

For function-based views, you can apply the decorator directly above the view definition.

```
@user_is_snippet_author

def edit_snippet(request, pk):
```

```
# View logic here
```

Testing Your Decorator

Ensure thorough testing of your decorator by creating unit tests that verify both the permitted and forbidden paths work as expected. This could involve mocking user requests to the decorated view and asserting the correct responses are returned based on the user's relationship to the snippet.

Recipe 5: Implementing Real-time Features using Django Channels

Scenario

With the introduction of real-time features like live notifications or real-time chat functionalities, GitforGits hopes to increase user engagement. Since real-time features necessitate long-lived, asynchronous connections, traditional Django is ill-suited to manage them. To bridge the gap and enable the development of asynchronous, real-time online applications, Django Channels enhances Django to support WebSockets, HTTP2, and other protocols.

Desired Solution

Setting Up Django Channels

To begin integrating real-time features, first install Django Channels in your virtual environment:

```
pip install channels
```

Add **channels** to your **INSTALLED_APPS** in **settings.py**, and specify Channels' development server as your default ASGI application server:

```
INSTALLED_APPS = [

 ...

 'channels',

]
```

```
ASGI_APPLICATION = 'gitforgits.routing.application'
```

Create a **routing.py** file in your project to define WebSocket routes, similar to how URLs are defined for HTTP routes in Django:

```
from channels.routing import ProtocolTypeRouter, URLRouter

from django.urls import path

from yourapp.consumers import MyConsumer

application = ProtocolTypeRouter({

 "websocket": URLRouter([

 path("ws/somepath/", MyConsumer.as_asgi()),

 ]),

})
```

Creating a Consumer

Consumers are Channels' equivalent of Django views – asynchronous handlers that manage WebSocket connections. Define a consumer that handles WebSocket events like connecting, receiving messages, and disconnecting:

```
from channels.generic.websocket import AsyncWebsocketConsumer

import json

class MyConsumer(AsyncWebsocketConsumer):

 async def connect(self):

 await self.accept()

 async def disconnect(self, close_code):

 pass
```

```
async def receive(self, text_data):
text_data_json = json.loads(text_data)
message = text_data_json['message']
await self.send(text_data=json.dumps({
'message': message
}))
```

This basic consumer accepts incoming WebSocket connections, echoes received messages back to the client, and handles disconnections.

Configuring Channels Layers

Channels layers are the communication system between consumers and are necessary for broadcasting messages to multiple consumers. Install Redis, a popular choice for a Channels layer backend, and configure it in **settings.py**:

```
CHANNEL_LAYERS = {
'default': {
'BACKEND': 'channels_redis.core.RedisChannelLayer',
'CONFIG': {
"hosts": [('127.0.0.1', 6379)],
},
},
}
```

Ensure Redis is running on your server or use a hosted Redis instance.

Front-end WebSocket Connection

In your front-end code, create a WebSocket connection to the server and handle incoming and outgoing messages:

```
var socket = new WebSocket('ws://' + window.location.host + '/ws/somepath/');
socket.onmessage = function(e) {
 var data = JSON.parse(e.data);
 var message = data['message'];
 // Handle message
};
socket.onclose = function(e) {
 console.error('Chat socket closed unexpectedly');
};
document.querySelector('#your-form-id').onsubmit = function(e) {
 var messageInputDom = document.querySelector('#your-message-input-id');
 var message = messageInputDom.value;
 socket.send(JSON.stringify({
 'message': message
 }));
 messageInputDom.value = '';
};
```

By incorporating Django Channels' real-time functionality, GitforGits gains a whole new level of engagement, letting users communicate, get notifications, and see updates as they happen in real time. The program can manage asynchronous, bidirectional communication by using WebSockets over Channels, which dramatically improves the user experience with real-time capabilities.

Recipe 6: Implementing WebSockets

Scenario

Expanding on our previous recipe of Django's real-time capabilities with Channels, we shall zero in on WebSockets implementation. With WebSockets, the server may push real-time changes to the client through a single, persistent connection that allows full-duplex communication. Use cases where the client doesn't need to explicitly request data from the server, such as live chat or real-time notifications, are ideal for this feature.

Desired Solution

Define WebSocket Routes in routing.py

Expand your **routing.py** file to include the WebSocket route for the feature you are implementing, such as a live chat. The **routing.py** file acts similarly to **urls.py** but for asynchronous protocols.

```
from django.urls import path

from channels.routing import ProtocolTypeRouter, URLRouter

from chat.consumers import ChatConsumer

application = ProtocolTypeRouter({

 'websocket': URLRouter([

 path('ws/chat/<room_name>/', ChatConsumer.as_asgi()),

 ]),

})
```

Create a WebSocket Consumer

Consumers handle the connection, disconnection, and communication over WebSockets. Given below is how you might implement a **ChatConsumer** for a live chat feature.

```
import json
```

```
from channels.generic.websocket import AsyncWebsocketConsumer
class ChatConsumer(AsyncWebsocketConsumer):
async def connect(self):
self.room_name = self.scope['url_route']['kwargs']['room_name']
self.room_group_name = f'chat_{self.room_name}'
# Join room group
await self.channel_layer.group_add(
self.room_group_name,
self.channel_name
)
await self.accept()
async def disconnect(self, close_code):
# Leave room group
await self.channel_layer.group_discard(
self.room_group_name,
self.channel_name
)
async def receive(self, text_data):
text_data_json = json.loads(text_data)
message = text_data_json['message']
```

```
# Send message to room group
await self.channel_layer.group_send(
self.room_group_name,
{
'type': 'chat_message',
'message': message,
}
)
# Receive message from room group
async def chat_message(self, event):
message = event['message']
# Send message to WebSocket
await self.send(text_data=json.dumps({
'message': message,
}))
```

Handling WebSocket Connections in the Frontend

Implement the logic to handle WebSocket connections in your client-side JavaScript. This includes connecting to the WebSocket, sending messages, and receiving updates from the server.

```
<script>
const roomName = JSON.parse(document.getElementById('room-name').textContent);
const chatSocket = new WebSocket(
```

```
'ws://' + window.location.host + '/ws/chat/' + roomName + '/'
);
chatSocket.onmessage = function(e) {
 const data = JSON.parse(e.data);
 document.querySelector('#chat-log').value += (data.message + '\n');
};
chatSocket.onclose = function(e) {
 console.error('Chat socket closed unexpectedly');
};
document.querySelector('#chat-message-input').onkeyup = function(e) {
 if (e.keyCode === 13) { // enter, return
 document.querySelector('#chat-message-submit').click();
 }
};
document.querySelector('#chat-message-submit').onclick = function(e) {
 const messageInputDom = document.querySelector('#chat-message-input');
 const message = messageInputDom.value;
 chatSocket.send(JSON.stringify({
 'message': message
 }));
 messageInputDom.value = '';
```

```
};
</script>
```

You can make your user experience really dynamic and engaging by using WebSockets in your Django app using Django Channels. This technique may be customized to work with various real-time features, making GitforGits even more useful and appealing.

Recipe 7: Performing Efficient Full-text Search with Django

Scenario

To keep users engaged and satisfied, it is essential that they can easily find the information they need. A more efficient and user-friendly search experience can be achieved by implementing full-text search, even if Django's ORM comes with excellent tools for database searches. Users can discover the most relevant results depending on their query using full-text search, which can completely search through vast volumes of text. With Django's PostgreSQL backend, you can do full-text searches, which open up a world of possibilities for advanced searching beyond keyword matching.

Desired Solution

Leverage PostgreSQL's Full-Text Search

Ensure your Django project's database is set up with PostgreSQL, as Django's full-text search functionality is particularly powerful with this backend, offering built-in support for full-text search without the need for external indexing services.

Update Models and Create a Search Vector

To implement full-text search, first, decide on the fields in your models that you want to be searchable. For instance, if you have a **Snippet** model with **title** and **description** fields, you can create a search vector for these fields.

Add a **SearchVectorField** to your model and create a migration to populate this field:

```
from django.contrib.postgres.search import SearchVectorField

from django.db import models
```

```
class Snippet(models.Model):
 title = models.CharField(max_length=100)
 description = models.TextField()
 search_vector = SearchVectorField(null=True)
 class Meta:
 indexes = [
 models.Index(fields=['search_vector']),
 ]
```

Run python manage.py makemigrations and python manage.py migrate to apply these changes.

Update Your Search Vector with Trigger

To automatically update the **search_vector** field whenever a **Snippet** is added or changed, use a PostgreSQL trigger. You can define this trigger in a migration:

```
from django.db import migrations
from django.contrib.postgres.operations import TrigramExtension
class Migration(migrations.Migration):
 dependencies = [
 ('yourapp', '0001_initial'),
 ]
 operations = [
 TrigramExtension(),
 migrations.RunSQL(
 """
```

```
 CREATE TRIGGER update_snippet_search_vector BEFORE INSERT OR
UPDATE

 ON yourapp_snippet FOR EACH ROW EXECUTE FUNCTION

 tsvector_update_trigger(search_vector, 'pg_catalog.english', title, description);

 """,

 "DROP TRIGGER update_snippet_search_vector ON yourapp_snippet;",

 ),

 ]
```

This sets up the trigger to update the **search_vector** using both the **title** and **description** fields of the **Snippet** model.

Performing Search Queries

With the search vector in place, you can now perform full-text searches against it. Modify your view to use Django's **SearchQuery**, **SearchRank**, and **SearchVector** to filter **Snippet** objects based on a search query:

```
from django.contrib.postgres.search import SearchQuery, SearchRank, SearchVector

from .models import Snippet

def search_snippets(request):

 query = request.GET.get('q', '')

 search_vector = SearchVector('title', weight='A') + SearchVector('description',
weight='B')

 search_query = SearchQuery(query)

 results = Snippet.objects.annotate(

 rank=SearchRank(search_vector, search_query)
```

```
).filter(rank__gte=0.3).order_by('-rank')

return render(request, 'snippets/search_results.html', {'results': results})
```

By leveraging PostgreSQL's built-in features, we can improve GitforGits' search functionality and make it even easier for users to locate what they're looking for. In addition to enhancing the user experience, this method makes advantage of PostgreSQL's powerful features to do away with third-party search engines.

Summary

This chapter explored improving GitforGits with advanced capabilities, showing Django's flexibility and strength for constructing complex, interactive web applications. In this chapter, we learned how to build responsive user interfaces using sophisticated AJAX techniques. These interfaces enhance the user experience by allowing content to be updated asynchronously. Thanks to this technique, the platform feels quicker and more natural, and the app can respond to user inputs in real time without requiring full page refreshes.

The chapter continued with the creation and administration of individual user profiles, which enabled a more tailored user experience by augmenting the default user model with extra data. In order to increase the platform's relevance and engagement, the process of creating dynamic content using Django templates demonstrated how to provide users with personalized content. As a further example of Django's capacity to encourage code reuse and maintainability, the introduction of building custom decorators for views simplified and standardized the deployment of common functionality across views, including logging or permission checks. The chapter continued with exploring real-time features utilizing Django Channels and WebSockets. These features allowed for realtime updates and interactions, including chat functionality, which significantly enhance user engagement and pleasure. Last but not least, it went over how to utilize Django to build efficient full-text search, showing how to harness database capabilities to provide strong search capabilities, making sure users can simply explore and access the platform's massive quantity of contents.

In sum, this chapter demonstrated how to integrate Django's sophisticated web application features into GitforGits and covered the actual, step-by-step process of doing so.

Chapter 10: Django and the Ecosystem

Introduction

This last and last chapter will walk you through the smooth integration of Django with the many tools and technologies that made up the modern web development ecosystem. By utilizing these integrations, the GitforGits program may significantly improve its architecture, user experience, and operational efficiency as it continues to mature. Web applications that are secure, scalable, and easy to maintain can be built using Django in conjunction with various front-end frameworks, deployment tools, and system architectures.

Starting with the most popular front-end JavaScript frameworks, React.js and Vue.js, and integrating Django with them is where the chapter begins. By integrating the reactive and component-driven features of React and Vue with Django's powerful back-end capabilities, these recipes will show how to build dynamic user interfaces. Developers may now take advantage of the best features of both ecosystems thanks to this integration, giving users an enhanced, personalized experience.

The use of containerization in conjunction with Docker and Django for Development and Production provides a way to standardize environments for testing, development, and production. Django developers can improve their apps' scalability, portability, and deployment speed by containerizing their applications. This also solves the "it works on my machine" problem. Accelerating releases and enhancing code quality through automated testing and deployment pipelines are two benefits of using CI/CD, which further automates the software development process.

An important part of maintaining and debugging live applications is logging their activity. In Logging Applications in Django, we will look at successful ways for doing just that. In order for developers to resolve issues, comprehend user interactions, and make educated judgments on future improvements, proper logging methods are essential. Addressing the difficulties of expanding web applications to fulfill rising demand is the focus of Scaling Django Applications with Distributed Systems. High availability and responsiveness can be achieved by dividing application load and data over different servers, which is explored in this recipe.

Lastly, the need of safeguarding sensitive data and guaranteeing secure server-client communications is emphasized in Securing Django APIs. To protect user data and application integrity, this recipe covers best practices and technologies for securing RESTful APIs. It includes authentication, authorization checks, and data encryption.

Recipe 1: Integrating Django with React.js

Scenario

Integrating a modern JavaScript framework like React.js with Django offers a tempting way to boost the application's interactivity and responsiveness. The component-based design provided by React.js makes it possible to create engaging UIs that are both functional and easy to use. Django apps that use React's quick update and rendering mechanism provide dynamic content with few page refreshes, giving the impression of a native app.

Desired Solution

Benefits of React to Django Apps

Integrating React with Django combines Django's robust backend capabilities with React's efficient, declarative, and flexible JavaScript library for building user interfaces. This integration allows for:

- Improved User Experience: React's virtual DOM and efficient update mechanisms provide a smoother, faster user experience by only rendering components that change.
- Modular Development: React's component-based approach facilitates reusable UI components, making development more organized and maintainable.
- Enhanced Scalability: React can handle complex user interfaces and large volumes of data, making it suitable for scaling your Django application.

Create a React App

Install Node.js and npm on your development machine if you haven't already. Inside your Django project directory, create a new React application using Create React App.

Run the following command:

```
npx create-react-app frontend
```

This command creates a new directory **frontend** with a boilerplate React application.

Integrate React with Django

Configure Django to serve the React app's static files. First, build your React app:

```
cd frontend

npm run build
```

This generates a **build** directory containing your static files and an **index.html**.

Serve these static files through Django by moving the **build** folder to your Django static files directory or by configuring Django's **STATICFILES_DIRS** to include the path to the

build/static directory.

Proxy API Requests During Development

To facilitate seamless integration between Django backend and React frontend during development, add a proxy to the React app's **package.json** to redirect API requests to Django's development server:

```
"proxy": "http://localhost:8000",
```

This setup helps in avoiding CORS issues during development by proxying API requests from React's development server (usually running on **localhost:3000**) to Django's server.

Run Both Servers

Start Django's development server:

```
python manage.py runserver
```

In a separate terminal, start the React development server:

```
cd frontend

npm start
```

For powerful, scalable, and dynamic web apps, always try integrating React.js with Django as above. The front end is improved by React's efficient rendering and component-based architecture, and the back end is maintained using Django.

Recipe 2: Integrating Django with Vue.js

Scenario

There have been talks of combining Django with the modern JavaScript framework Vue.js in order to make GitforGits even better for users. Web pages can become much more interactive and responsive with Vue's reactive data binding and component-based architecture, which in turn makes for a more engaging user experience.

Desired Solution

Benefits of Vue to Django Apps

Vue.js complements Django by bringing a modern, component-based approach to the frontend, allowing for the development of rich interactive UIs with less overhead. Its main advantages include:

- Ease of Integration: Vue can be easily integrated into Django templates, enhancing parts of your application with complex behaviors or as a SPA (Single Page Application) for more interactive experiences.
- Reactivity: Vue's reactive data binding system automatically updates the DOM when the state of the application changes, simplifying the development of dynamic interfaces.
- Flexibility: Vue's ecosystem provides tools and libraries for state management, routing, and more, making it adaptable to a wide range of project requirements.

Setting up Vue

- Install Node.js and npm if not already installed. Node.js will be used to run the Vue CLI and manage project dependencies.
- Use Vue CLI to create a new Vue project within your Django project directory. Open a terminal, navigate to your Django project directory, and run:

```
npm install -g @vue/cli

vue create frontend
```

When prompted, select the default preset or manually select features for your Vue application.

Configure Vue to Work with Django

In the Vue project directory (**frontend**), locate **vue.config.js**. If it doesn't exist, create it. Configure it to output the build files to a directory that Django can serve:

```
module.exports = {

 outputDir: '../static/frontend',

 indexPath: '../../templates/frontend/index.html',

 devServer: {

 proxy: {
```

```
'/api': {
 target: 'http://localhost:8000',
 changeOrigin: true,
 },
 },
 },
};
```

This setup directs Vue to place built static files in Django's **static** directory and the entry HTML file in Django's **templates** directory. The **devServer** proxy forwards API requests to Django during development, helping to avoid CORS issues.

Build the Vue App

Build your Vue application to generate static files:

```
cd frontend
npm run build
```

Serving Vue with Django

Ensure Django's **settings.py** is configured to find the Vue static files and the entry **index.html**:

```
STATICFILES_DIRS = [
 os.path.join(BASE_DIR, 'static'),
]
TEMPLATES = [
 {
 ...
```

```
'DIRS': [os.path.join(BASE_DIR, 'templates')],
...
},
]
```

You can serve the Vue app's entry point (**index.html**) through a Django view or directly use it as a template for a Django URL route.

Running Your Application

Start the Django development server with following command:

```
python manage.py runserver
```

For development, run Vue's development server alongside Django's server:

```
npm run serve
```

A potent mix for developing dynamic, responsive web apps is Vue.js with Django integrated. By integrating Django's server-side logic with Vue's robust client-side functionality, developers can take advantage of the best features of both frameworks.

Recipe 3: Using Docker with Django for Development and Production

Scenario

To reduce "it works only on my machine" problems and simplify deployment procedures, it is critical to ensure consistency across development, testing, and production environments. You can find that solution with Docker. To facilitate deployment and scaling, Docker can containerize the Django application together with all of its dependencies and environment-specific settings. This encapsulates the application in a consistent environment from development to production.

Desired Solution

Benefits of Docker to Django Apps

- Environment Consistency: Docker containers ensure that your application runs in the same environment regardless of where the container is deployed, reducing discrepancies between development, testing, and production.
- Simplified Dependency Management: All dependencies are included within the container, eliminating the need for manual environment setup.
- Ease of Deployment and Scaling: Containers can be easily started, stopped, and scaled across machines and cloud environments.

Create a Dockerfile

Ensure Docker and Docker Compose are installed on your development machine. Installation guides are available on the Docker website. After that, in your Django project root, create a **Dockerfile** that defines how to build your Docker container. Given below is a simple example:

```
# Use an official Python runtime as a parent image

FROM python:3.8

# Set environment variables

ENV PYTHONUNBUFFERED 1

# Set the working directory in the container

WORKDIR /app

# Copy the current directory contents into the container at /app

COPY . /app

# Install any needed packages specified in requirements.txt

RUN pip install --upgrade pip && pip install -r requirements.txt

# Make port 8000 available to the world outside this container

EXPOSE 8000

# Define environment variable
```

```
ENV NAME World

# Run `python manage.py runserver 0.0.0.0:8000` when the container launches

CMD ["python", "manage.py", "runserver", "0.0.0.0:8000"]
```

Define Services in a docker-compose.yml File

To manage your application alongside other services such as a database, create a **docker-compose.yml** file. This file defines the services, networks, and volumes for your Dockerized environment.

```
version: '3'

services:

 db:

 image: postgres

 environment:

 POSTGRES_DB: gitforgits

 POSTGRES_USER: user

 POSTGRES_PASSWORD: password

 web:

 build: .

 command: python manage.py runserver 0.0.0.0:8000

 volumes:

 - .:/app

 ports:

 - "8000:8000"
```

```
depends_on:

- db
```

This configuration sets up a PostgreSQL database and your Django application as services, ensuring they can communicate with each other.

Build and Run Your Containers

With your **Dockerfile** and **docker-compose.yml** in place, build your Docker image and start your services:

```
docker-compose build

docker-compose up
```

This will start your Django application and database in containers, accessible at **localhost:8000**.

Migrate and Create a Superuser

Run migrations and create a superuser for your Django admin:

```
docker-compose run web python manage.py migrate

docker-compose run web python manage.py createsuperuser
```

With this docker strategy, changes made to the Dockerfile or docker-compose configurations are simply propagated through CI/CD pipelines, ensuring consistency throughout development and simplifying scalability and upgrades.

Recipe 4: Implementing Continuous Integration and Continuous Deployment (CI/CD)

Scenario

CI/CD allows for the automated testing of code changes in a shared repository and deployment to production environments, ensuring that updates are delivered quickly and reliably. Using the

Dockerized environment we created in the previous recipe in conjunction with Jenkins, we can build a CI/CD pipeline for Django apps.

Desired Solution

Benefits of CI/CD for Django Apps

- Automated Testing: Automatically run tests on every commit, ensuring that new changes don't break existing functionality.
- Rapid Feedback: Developers receive immediate feedback on their changes, enabling quick iterations and improvements.
- Consistent Deployments: Automated deployments reduce manual errors, ensuring that the application is deployed consistently across environments.

Install Jenkins

If Jenkins isn't already installed, set it up on a server or locally. Jenkins can be containerized, making it compatible with your Dockerized Django project. For simplicity, you can run Jenkins in a Docker container:

```
docker run -d -p 8080:8080 -p 50000:50000 -v jenkins_home:/var/jenkins_home
jenkins/jenkins:lts
```

Once Jenkins is running, navigate to **http://localhost:8080** and complete the initial setup using the instructions provided.

Configure Jenkins with Git

- Create a new "Freestyle project" in Jenkins for your GitforGits repository.
- Under the Source Code Management section, enter your repository URL and credentials if it is private.
- Configure build triggers according to your preferences, such as triggering a build on every push to the repository.

Create Build and Test Steps

Use Jenkins to automate the testing of your Django application. In the Build section, add a step to pull your latest code, build your Docker containers, and run tests:

```
#!/bin/bash
```

```
docker-compose -f docker-compose.ci.yml build

docker-compose -f docker-compose.ci.yml up -d

docker-compose -f docker-compose.ci.yml run web python manage.py test
```

You may need a separate **docker-compose.ci.yml** that is configured for the CI environment, especially for services like databases.

Automate Deployment

After successful tests, automate the deployment of your application. This could involve SSHing into your production server and pulling the latest changes or using a tool like Docker Swarm or Kubernetes for orchestration.

For Jenkins, you can add a post-build action to deploy your application upon a successful build. The specifics of this step depend on your production environment and deployment strategy.

Monitor and Iterate

Monitor your Jenkins pipeline for any failures and optimize the process as needed. Jenkins provides detailed logs of each build and test run, which can be invaluable for diagnosing issues.

By promoting best practices such as test-driven development and continuous feedback, this setup significantly enhances code quality and makes projects much easier to manage. With the help of Jenkins and Docker, the CI/CD pipeline builds a solid foundation for GitforGits, making it possible for the platform to adapt quickly and securely to changing needs and user input.

Recipe 5: Using Prometheus to Log Django Apps

Scenario

For an application to stay healthy, logging and monitoring are essential. The open-source monitoring and alerting tool, Prometheus, has a stellar reputation for its robust data model, query language, and integration capabilities. With the help of Prometheus and Django, you can keep tabs on all the important metrics of your application, like request latency and system utilization. This will provide you the information you need to make your service more reliable and efficient.

Desired Solution

Introduction to Prometheus

Prometheus is designed for reliability and efficiency, primarily targeting dynamic service-oriented architectures. At its core, Prometheus scrapes metrics from configured targets at specified intervals, evaluates rule expressions, displays results, and can trigger alerts if certain conditions are met. Its querying language, PromQL, allows for precise, real-time monitoring of application behavior and performance. Prometheus's architecture and ecosystem include various components, such as exporters that expose metrics from non-Prometheus systems, client libraries for instrumenting application code, and an alert manager to handle alerts.

Installing Prometheus

For development purposes, you can run Prometheus locally. Download the latest release from the Prometheus website and extract it. Inside the extracted directory, edit the **prometheus.yml** configuration file to define the scrape targets, including your Django application.

Alternatively, run Prometheus in a Docker container for easier setup and integration with your existing Dockerized Django environment:

```
docker run -d -p 9090:9090 -v
/path/to/your/prometheus.yml:/etc/prometheus/prometheus.yml prom/prometheus
```

Replace **/path/to/your/prometheus.yml** with the path to your configuration file.

Instrumenting Your Django Application

To expose Django metrics to Prometheus, use the **django-prometheus** library. Install it in your Django environment:

```
pip install django-prometheus
```

Integrate **django-prometheus** middleware into your Django project by adding it to the **MIDDLEWARE** setting in your **settings.py**:

```
MIDDLEWARE = [

'django_prometheus.middleware.PrometheusBeforeMiddleware',

# Your other middleware classes

'django_prometheus.middleware.PrometheusAfterMiddleware',
```

```
]
```

Configure your **urls.py** to expose the metrics endpoint:

```
from django.urls import path, include


urlpatterns = [
 path('', include('django_prometheus.urls')),
 # Your other URL patterns
]
```

This setup will expose an endpoint (typically **/metrics**) that Prometheus can scrape to collect metrics from your Django application.

Configuring Prometheus to Scrape Django Metrics

In your **prometheus.yml**, add a new scrape job for your Django application:

```
scrape_configs:
 - job_name: 'django'
 static_configs:
 - targets: ['localhost:8000']
 metrics_path: '/metrics'
```

Adjust the **targets** value if your Django application is running on a different host or port.

Monitoring and Querying Metrics

With Prometheus running and configured to scrape metrics from your Django app, access the Prometheus web UI (usually available at **http://localhost:9090**) to start querying your application metrics using PromQL. This visibility from Prometheus is crucial for proactive performance tuning, troubleshooting issues, and ensuring that the application remains responsive and reliable with ever-growing user traffic.

Recipe 6: Containerizing Django Apps with Kubernetes on AWS

Scenario

When it comes to scaling, Kubernetes, an open-source platform for managing containerized applications, provides strong features for automation of deployment, scaling, and scaling. If you use Kubernetes, you can deploy any software to any number of servers, handle problems automatically, and scale up or down as needed. EKS, Amazon Web Services' managed Kubernetes offering, streamlines cluster management and interoperability with other AWS services.

Desired Solution

Introduction to Kubernetes

Kubernetes orchestrates containers across a cluster of machines, making it easier to deploy and manage applications at scale. It handles tasks such as automatic binpacking, self-healing (restarting failed containers), scaling, and rolling updates. Kubernetes introduces abstractions like Pods, Services, and Deployments to manage applications.

Setup the AWS CLI and eksctl

Ensure the AWS CLI is installed and configured with your credentials. Additionally, install **eksctl**, a simple CLI tool for creating clusters on EKS. It simplifies much of the cluster creation process.

```
brew install eksctl
```

Create an EKS Cluster

Use **eksctl** to create your cluster. This might take several minutes:

```
eksctl create cluster --name gitforgits-cluster --region us-west-2
```

This command creates an EKS cluster named **gitforgits-cluster** in the **us-west-2** region with default settings, which include managed node groups for your containers.

Containerize Your Django Application

Assuming you've already Dockerized your Django application (as covered in a previous recipe), ensure your **Dockerfile** is up to date and that your Docker image is built and pushed to a container registry like Amazon Elastic Container Registry (ECR).

Create a Kubernetes Deployment

A Deployment tells Kubernetes how to create and update instances of your application. Create a **django-deployment.yaml** file:

```
apiVersion: apps/v1
kind: Deployment
metadata:
 name: gitforgits-deployment
spec:
 replicas: 3
 selector:
 matchLabels:
 app: gitforgits
 template:
 metadata:
 labels:
 app: gitforgits
 spec:
 containers:
 - name: gitforgits
 image: <aws_account_id>.dkr.ecr.<region>.amazonaws.com/gitforgits:latest
```

```
 ports:
 - containerPort: 8000
```

Replace **<aws_account_id>** and **<region>** with your AWS account ID and the region where your ECR repository is hosted.

Deploy to Kubernetes

Apply the deployment configuration to your cluster:

```
kubectl apply -f django-deployment.yaml
```

Expose Your Django Application

Use a Kubernetes Service to expose your Django application to the internet:

```
apiVersion: v1
kind: Service
metadata:
 name: gitforgits-service
spec:
 type: LoadBalancer
 ports:
 - port: 80
 targetPort: 8000
 protocol: TCP
 selector:
 app: gitforgits
```

Apply this service configuration with **kubectl apply**.

Access Your Application

After the service is created, get the public IP address or hostname:

```
kubectl get services
```

Access your Django application via the provided IP or hostname. This setup ensures that GitforGits can efficiently manage resources, scale based on traffic, and maintain high availability, providing a seamless experience for its users.

Recipe 7: Securing Django APIs

Scenario

There are several serious dangers that can result from security breaches, including data leaks and illegal access. In order to comply with rules, safeguard sensitive data, and keep users' trust, strong security measures must be implemented.

Desired Solution

Use HTTPS

Ensure all API communications occur over HTTPS to encrypt data in transit. This prevents man-in-the-middle attacks and eavesdropping. If you haven't already, set up SSL/TLS certificates for your domain. Services like Let's Encrypt offer them for free.

Implement Token Authentication

DRF provides several authentication schemes, with token authentication being a popular choice for APIs. Tokens are unique to each user and must be included in the headers of HTTP requests to access protected resources.

```
INSTALLED_APPS = [

 ...

'rest_framework.authtoken',

 ...
```

```
]
```

Run **python manage.py migrate** to create the token model. Update your DRF settings in **settings.py** to use token authentication:

```
REST_FRAMEWORK = {
 'DEFAULT_AUTHENTICATION_CLASSES': [
 'rest_framework.authentication.TokenAuthentication',
 ],
}
```

Create a view to handle token requests, typically after a user logs in.

Permissions

Define permissions to restrict access to certain actions within your API. DRF allows you to set permissions globally or per-view, ensuring that only authorized users can perform sensitive operations.

```
REST_FRAMEWORK = {
 'DEFAULT_PERMISSION_CLASSES': [
 'rest_framework.permissions.IsAuthenticated',
 ],
}
```

Input Validation and Serialization

Properly validate all incoming data to prevent injection attacks and ensure the data conforms to expected formats. Use DRF serializers to automatically handle input validation.

```
from rest_framework import serializers
from .models import Snippet
```

```
class SnippetSerializer(serializers.ModelSerializer):
 class Meta:
 model = Snippet
 fields = ['id', 'title', 'code']
 extra_kwargs = {'title': {'required': True}}
```

Throttling

Protect your API from abuse and denial-of-service attacks by implementing throttling, limiting the number of requests a user can make in a given timeframe.

```
REST_FRAMEWORK = {
 ...
 'DEFAULT_THROTTLE_CLASSES': [
 'rest_framework.throttling.AnonRateThrottle',
 'rest_framework.throttling.UserRateThrottle'
 ],
 'DEFAULT_THROTTLE_RATES': {
 'anon': '100/day',
 'user': '1000/day'
 }
}
```

Regularly audit your API for new vulnerabilities and keep your dependencies updated. Tools like **safety** can help identify security issues in installed packages. Security is an ongoing process, requiring regular reviews and updates to address emerging vulnerabilities and threats.

Summary

Finally, this chapter demonstrated how GitforGits may expand its reach by integrating Django with key technologies and practices in the current web development environment. This chapter outlined a systematic strategy to improve the Django framework's capabilities, meeting changing requirements for interaction, scalability, security, and operational efficiency. Beginning with the integration of front-end frameworks React.js and Vue.js, the recipes demonstrated how to combine Django's powerful backend with dynamic and reactive user interfaces, raising the user experience to new heights. These integrations not only resulted in a modular and stable codebase, but they also utilised the characteristics of each framework to provide rich, client-side apps that are both performant and scalable.

Later, the chapter covered containerization with Docker and orchestration with Kubernetes, emphasizing the significance of consistency, portability, and scalability in application deployment and administration. By containerizing GitforGits, the application gained simpler development workflows, improved collaboration, and the ability to easily scale and deploy across many environments, all while maintaining a high level of dependability and availability. Furthermore, the introduction of Continuous Integration and Continuous Deployment approaches, aided by tools such as Jenkins, automated the testing and deployment processes, dramatically reducing change lead time and improving overall application quality. The emphasis on logging using Prometheus and securing Django APIs encapsulated the important parts of monitoring and security, guaranteeing that GitforGits not only runs well but also remains secure against evolving cyber threats. These measures gave significant insights into application performance and user behavior, as well as strengthened the application's defense mechanisms against unwanted access and data breaches.

Index

V

Epilogue

As we come to a close on this extensive exploration of Django and its place in the web development ecosystem, I pause to think about all we've accomplished together. If you're brave enough to dive into the complexities of web development with Django, this book will be there to help you every step of the way. It was formed out of a combination of experience, curiosity, and a strong desire to share what I've learned. Our journey has been educational and illuminating, covering everything from the basics of creating a Django project to the intricacies of releasing scalable web apps.

At the center of our book was the fictional but symbolic project GitforGits, which has served as a platform for learning django, representing the ups and downs of real-world progress. We have explored Django's intricacies and discovered its strength, adaptability, and grace through it. Not only are the recipes and scenarios presented here meant to teach you something, but they also aim to motivate you to think beyond the box and see what else Django can do.

The significance of being able to adapt in today's constantly changing tech landscape has been highlighted by the integration of Django with technologies like React.js, Vue.js, Docker, and Kubernetes. We went above and beyond what was previously possible in web development by using CI/CD principles, protecting APIs, and establishing distributed systems to guarantee great performance. These chapters demonstrate how Django and its ecosystem operate hand in hand, showcasing how the framework can adapt to and thrive in all types of contexts.

With the knowledge and abilities, you've gained from this book, you can continue your journey with Django. There are always fresh obstacles and opportunities in the ever-changing landscape of web development. I hope you'll never stop wondering how things work and will always be on the lookout for new methods to improve your apps and processes. Participate in group activities, make contributions to open source, and teach others what you've learned. You can never stop learning, and every obstacle you overcome will only serve to enhance your skills and knowledge.

To conclude, I want to express my deepest appreciation for the opportunity to accompany you on your Django adventure. I hope this book has been an invaluable resource for you as you work to become an expert Django developer, whether it has ignited a passion for web programming, strengthened your current abilities, or given you fresh ideas on how to tackle problems. Innovation, creativity, and inspiration abound on the path that lies ahead. As you continue to shape the digital world with your ideas and endeavors, may the wisdom gained and the stories told on these pages serve as a compass.

However, although though GitforGits is coming to an end, your journey is only just starting. Embrace the journey, treasure the lessons, and may your pursuit of personal growth take you somewhere you've never imagined. In the endlessly exciting realm of web development, here's to innumerable lines of code, creative apps, and the relentless quest of perfection.

Thank You

www.ingramcontent.com/pod-product-compliance
Lightning Source LLC
Chambersburg PA
CBHW080212170726
48282CB00030B/1090
9788119177677